James C. Harrison

HOOKED ON FITNESS!

FUN
Physical Conditioning Games and Activities for Grades K-8

PARKER PUBLISHING COMPANY
West Nyack, New York 10995

Library of Congress Cataloging-in-Publication Data

Harrison, James C.
 Hooked on fitness! : fun physical conditioning games & activities
for grades K-8 / James C. Harrison.
  p. cm.
 ISBN 0-13-065616-X : Spiral   ISBN 0-13-255902-1 : Paper
 1. Physical education for children. 2. Movement for children. I.
Title.
GV443.H32   1993
372.86—dc20

93-14314
CIP

Printed in the United States of America

10 9 8 7 6 5 4 (S)   *10 9 8 7 6 5 4 3 2 1 (P)*

ISBN 0-13-065616-X (S)   ISBN 0-13-255902-1 (P)

PARKER PUBLISHING COMPANY
West Nyack, NY 10994

A Simon & Schuster Company

On the World Wide Web at http://www.phdirect.com

Prentice-Hall International (UK) Limited, *London*
Prentice-Hall of Australia Pty. Limited, *Sydney*
Prentice-Hall Canada Inc., *Toronto*
Prentice-Hall Hispanoamericana, S.A., *Mexico*
Prentice-Hall of India Private Limited, *New Delhi*
Prentice-Hall of Japan, Inc., *Tokyo*
Simon & Schuster Asia Pte. Ltd., *Singapore*
Editora Prentice-Hall do Brasil, Ltda., *Rio de Janeiro*

DEDICATION

This book is dedicated to my daughters,
Christine and Wendy.

ACKNOWLEDGMENTS

I would like to thank my fellow teachers in Baltimore County whose responses and enthusiasm during inservice and staff development sessions encouraged me to write this book. Special thanks to my long-time friend Zack Karantonis for this assistance with some of the activities, but mostly for serving as my mentor in my early teaching years. Thanks also to fellow teacher Sandi Stevens who tried out many of these activities and gave constructive suggestions. A special thank you to Bob Melville who gave insight from a supervisor's perspective. And thanks especially to Rose Marie Trimeloni who had the difficult task of taking the ramblings of an ideas person and rewording them so they made sense and were readable, and without whose patience, understanding, and assistance this book would not have been possible.

ABOUT THE AUTHOR

James C. Harrison (M.S., Morgan State University; B.S., Towson State University), has been a physical education teacher at the elementary level in Baltimore County, Maryland for over 20 years. Jim has taught numerous inservice courses and staff-development sessions throughout Maryland. In addition, he has created and written an inservice course on cooperative and initiative activities, and served as a member of the committee that wrote the current "Physical Education Curriculum Guide" used in Baltimore County. Since 1988 he has taught college courses at Essex Community College in aerobic fitness and beginner tennis. As a member of the committee that organizes the Board of Education Annual Walk-Run for Fitness for 2,000 employees, he is responsible for the course design and finish line. Jim is also director of the largest annual kids' running race in the area, the Kids' Classic, at Goucher College. He is the father of two daughters, Christine and Wendy.

A competitive athlete for over 33 years, Jim has earned hundreds of awards and honors, including the Towson State College Athlete of the Year (1972), Masters Runner of the Year in Baltimore four years in a row (in the 1980s), winner of the Air Force tennis and squash championship (1968), winner of the first triathlon ever held east of the Mississippi (1979), and twice finished in the top ten of his age group in the triathlon national championship, earning All-American honors in 1989.

ABOUT THIS BOOK

We are being told that kids are different today, that physically they are not as fit as past generations. It's the age of the computer, and kids just don't play like they used to. It's TV and video games, not bicycles and roller skates. But society has also changed and some of these changes make active play less likely to be a part of everyday life. Increasing pollution, unsafe streets, parents absent from home during potential play hours, lack of adequate recreational facilities, reliance on air conditioning, and passive transportation all make active play less attractive than in the past.

The job of educators must also change. Traditional activities, as well as new ones, need to be modified to become more exciting and challenging—so that kids enjoy playing them—and more active—so that kids become fitter and learn to enjoy vigorous movement. *Hooked on Fitness! Fun Physical Conditioning Games and Activities for Grades K-8* will help you do this.

The two greatest physical needs of kids, according to fitness test results, are aerobic conditioning and upper body strength. And the greatest desire of all kids is to have fun. This book is filled with activities to help develop these fitness components in a way that makes play exciting. Having kids run a mile or so in class might be good for their bodies, but may, in fact, turn them away from a valuable activity; whereas, participation in an aerobic game, like Swatball, is fun and more suitable to a child's natural way of moving. This book's focus is on enjoyment of active play. Seldom would kids enjoy 15 to 20 minutes of continuous movement (as needed by adults for a cardio-vascular workout); studies show that children prefer stop-and-start activities rather than continuous movement.

You'll find over 100 conditioning games and activities in *Hooked on Fitness!*, as well as directions for making equipment, instructions for designing Sports Days, and ready-to-use forms and fitness tests.

Each fitness game and activity provides you with:

❏ the appropriate grade level

❏ a brief description

❏ its objective

❏ a list of the equipment you'll need

❐ easy-to-follow directions and illustrations

❐ additional suggestions and variations

The games and activities will also indicate whether they are geared to be "less active," "active," "very active," or to develop "strength."

Research tells us that as little as five minutes of aerobic exercise will elicit cardio-vascular conditioning, provided the pulse rate is at a fairly high level. Having done mid-game pulse checks, I've found these games and activities to be aerobic in nature. Games should last a minimum of five minutes, if possible. During play, children have the opportunity to self-pace. The very fit child will play vigorously, while a less fit child might play at a less active pace. Each child will develop at his or her own pace.

The primary goals of physical education in grades K-8 are to create an enjoyment of movement, to acquire the basic skills and fitness with which to be successful in play, and to be aware of the basic concepts of fitness. *Fun is what kids want most; fitness is what they need most.* Combine these elements—and you and your kids will be "hooked on fitness"!

James C. Harrison

CONTENTS

Section 3 / ACTIVE GAMES • 43

Section 4 / STRENGTH ACTIVITIES • 121

Section 5 / ACTIVE STATIONS • 161

Section 6 / HOT-WEATHER STATIONS • 171

Section 7 / THINGS TO MAKE • 179

Section 8 / ACTIVE SPORTS-DAY DESIGNS • 225

Section 9 / FITNESS TESTING • 235

Section 10 / READY-TO-USE FORMS • 239

LIST OF ACTIVITIES • 253

AEROBIC WARM-UPS

Here are eleven aerobic warm-ups that can be used often to begin a class. Try to include some kind of vigorous activity, such as these, in every class, especially if the lesson for that day is not very active.

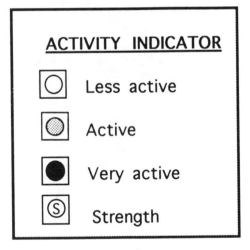

1.1 AEROBIC MATH

Grade Level: K-2

Description: A sort of musical chairs warm-up that teaches or reinforces math skills while developing open space running and locomotor skills.

Objective: To quickly get into a group of the designated number so as not to be eliminated.

Equipment: Gym or field

Directions:

1. Explain that on the signal "Go", students will run randomly about the area without touching one another.

2. The teacher will call out a number. Students are to quickly form groups of that number.

3. Any students not in a group of that number by the signal "Stop" must sit out one turn. Allow a reasonable time for grouping. Having too few or too many people in a group are equally wrong.

4. Any players sitting out are invited back on the next round.

Suggestions:

❏ Begin with easy numbers and increase the difficulty in order to challenge students.

❏ Encourage safe running and stopping.

❏ To start the next round, call out, "Hop", "Skip" or other locomotor skills instead of running.

Variations:

1. Instead of calling out a number, tell students that a certain number of whistle blasts will sound. Form groups equal to that number.

2. Call out math problems, such as "Five plus two" to get groups of seven or "Five minus two, plus one" for groups of four.

1.2 DRIBBLE TAG

Grade Level: 3-8

Description: A basketball warm-up activity for the whole class that improves cardio-vascular systems as well as dribbling skills.

Objective: To maintain control of your dribbling basketball while simultaneously attempting to swat away basketballs from other dribblers.

Equipment: 1 basketball (or any suitable ball for dribbling) per person

Directions:

1. Distribute one ball to each participant.

2. Explain the **rule:**
   Participants must maintain control of their balls to remain active players. If they lose control (or have their ball swatted away), they must regain control before again attempting to swat away balls. No one is ever "out"; they just regain control and continue.

Suggestion:

❑ Students will naturally change hands, pivot away from attackers, and use their body to shield the ball—all of which are desirable dribbling skills.

1.3 LACROSSE FACE-OFF DRILL

Grade Level: 3-8

Description: A needed skill in the game of lacrosse that is made into a competitive warm-up.

Objective: To be the first to get the ball into your stick.

Equipment: STX lacrosse sticks and balls (or use tennis balls)

Directions:

1. Explain that, in lacrosse, play is started with a face-off. Face-offs are important because the team that wins the face-off gets control of the ball first.

2. Demonstrate face-off and discuss the rules:
   a. The ball is placed on the ground. Both players place the backs of their sticks against the ball. The knuckles of their hands are placed on the ground. Players may be kneeling or standing.
   b. When the contest begins, both players attempt to get the ball into their "cross" (the catching part of the stick). They may kick the ball away and use their bodies to block out the opponent. However, they may not dislodge the ball once the other player gets the ball into his or her cross.

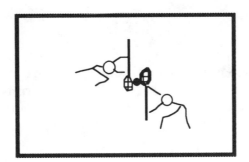

Suggestion:

❐ Have players hold up the "W" or "L" sign with their hands (signifying win or loss) after each contest to look for another player with the same sign to be the next opponent.

1.4 REVOLVING DOOR

Grade Level: 3-8

Description: A team jump rope activity for indoor or outdoor.

Objective: To have as many group members as possible go through the turning rope before a mistake is made.

Equipment: 1 long jump rope per group

Directions:

1. Divide the class into groups of ten or more with two people selected as turners.

2. The group lines up perpendicular to the turning rope (the rope should be turning "front door"; that is, turning toward the top of the jumpers' heads, not their feet).

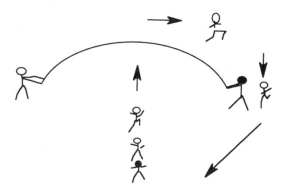

3. Participants attempt to run through the turning rope one at a time with one jumper going through with each turn of the rope. NOTE: If more than one jumper goes through on one turn of the rope, or if a jumper fails to go through each time the rope comes around, the count for that group's effort is stopped.

4. Allow many attempts to record the group's highest score. Record the best effort.

Suggestions:

❏ This may be done as a whole class activity or, for more action, divide the class into two or three smaller groups.

❐ Timing is most important. Jumpers should keep moving forward in the line so they are very close to the turning rope. The rope hitting the floor becomes an auditory signal for the next jumper to go. Each time the rope hits the floor, a jumper should quickly start through the turning rope.

❐ Post the groups' best scores on the gym wall to recognize their efforts or post the scores of all classes in "Revolving Door."

Variation:

For a more difficult challenge, have each participant jump the turning rope *one time* before exiting out the other side of the turning rope.

1.5 RUN AND ROLL

Grade Level: K-8

Description: An active warm-up for gymnastics that combines running and rolling to ready the body for more advanced gymnastics.

Objective: To practice the shoulder roll (or safety roll) while running as a warm-up.

Equipment: Tumbling mats

Directions:

1. Review how to perform a shoulder roll. NOTE: A shoulder roll is similar to a forward roll except that one shoulder is tucked under so that the roll is done across that shoulder and diagonally across the back to the opposite hip, as opposed to straight down the back. The head should **not** touch the mat in a shoulder roll.

2. Instruct students to begin jogging around the room looking for **open** mats on which they will practice a shoulder roll and then jog to other mats, repeating more shoulder rolls. Or if the class responds better to a little more structure, designate a one-way pattern on all mats.

Suggestions:

❒ The shoulder or safety roll is a very important protection skill. During this warm-up, assist students who have difficulty performing this skill correctly. Safe falling must become an unconscious, automatic reaction if it is to prevent injuries.

❒ Place a folded mat, inner tube, or other soft object on the mat for a diving shoulder roll.

❒ Used at the beginning of class, students develop good falling habits that may be needed in class. The shoulder roll is the preferred way to fall when the body is going head first toward a crash. The back and shoulders can take much more impact than can the head, knees, spine, etc.

1.6 SCOOP AND DROP DRILL

Grade Level: 1-8

Description: A competitive lacrosse drill that practices the skills of picking up a lacrosse ball with the stick.

Objective: To help your team pick up and drop the most balls into your team's barrel.

Equipment: STX lacrosse sticks, 60 or more tennis balls or soft lacrosse balls; 2 standard trash barrels or boxes

Directions:

1. Divide the class into two teams.

2. Distribute a different color stick to all players on each team.

3. Demonstrate the two methods of picking up a lacrosse ball.

    a. *Scooping*—The preferred way to pick up a ball. The player holds the stick with both hands. Using a motion similar to shoveling snow and keeping the hands close to the ground, the player scoops through the ball and lifts up.

    b. *Raking*—The player places the back of the stick on top of the ball and pulls the ball back towards him or her and then lifts the stick up.

4. Scatter balls throughout the area.

5. On signal, all players attempt to scoop or rake **one ball at a time** and run to their barrel, depositing the ball.

6. Select a player to count the number of balls his or her team has collected.

7. Repeat several times.

Suggestions:

❐ Encourage scooping rather than raking.

❐ No player may try to dislodge a ball from a lacrosse stick.

1.7 SOCCER CROSS COUNTRY

Grade Level: K-8

Description: This warm-up combines jogging with soccer dribbling. Simply adding a ball makes each participant a "Funner Runner."

Objective: To control a soccer ball as you dribble around a running course.

Equipment: 1 ball per person; a running course

Directions:

1. Distribute one ball to each student.

2. Describe the running course. This can be the regular cross country course (including up and down hills) or just around the soccer field area.

3. Give students a skill (such as heading) to begin working on when they finish the course.

Variations:

❏ *Football Lateral Jog:* (Grade 3 and up): In this version, two students lateral a football between themselves as they jog. Demonstrate or remind students that a lateral pass must be made underhand and backward to the partner.

❏ *Lacrosse Jog and Cradle:* Students jog with a tennis ball or soft lacrosse ball held in their lacrosse stick. While jogging, they practice a "cradling" motion with the head of the stick. This rhythmic motion helps keep the ball from falling out of the stick.

1.8 SPEED SHOOTING RACE

Grade Level: 3-8

Description: A way to increase both heart rate and speed shooting abilities. It is used as a basketball warm-up.

Objective: To shoot as quickly as possible all of the designated baskets.

Equipment: As many baskets as you have; 1 ball per player

Directions:

1. Set up as many baskets as you have. If you don't have many baskets, require two shots at each basket for more action, or assign a designated number of total baskets to be shot. About 10-12 baskets is a good number.

2. Explain the **rule:**
   Each participant must successfully shoot each basket (in any desired order).

3. Upon finishing, each player goes to a designated location.

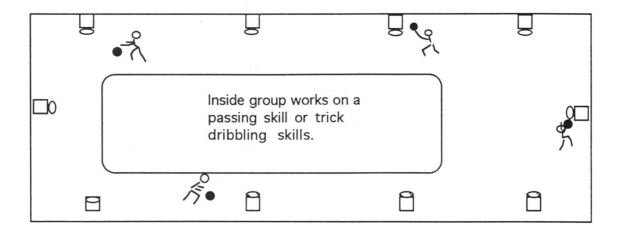

Inside group works on a passing skill or trick dribbling skills.

Suggestions:

❏ Since baskets are usually set up around the gym, have an alternate activity for half the class in the center of the gym (for example, a passing or dribbling activity). While one group does the shooting race, the other group does the dribbling drill—then groups switch activities.

❏ Put out three blocks on the floor with the numbers 1-2-3 on them (or put numbers directly on the floor). The first finisher stands on the #1 spot, the second finisher stands on #2, etc.

❏ You might want to limit the maximum number of shots tried at a basket. If a player doesn't score after about five attempts, he or she moves to the next basket anyway. This prevents a player from finishing way behind the others or getting frustrated.

1.9 TENNIS BALL JOG

Grade Level: K-8

Description: An activity that expresses the importance of keeping fitness fun. It can be done indoor or outdoor.

Objective: To combine jogging and playing with a ball.

Equipment: 1 tennis ball per person

Directions:

1. Tell the story (true, by the way) of a runner who one day found a tennis ball while running. Thinking to take it home to his dog, he picked it up. After a short while he grew tired of carrying the ball so he began tossing the ball and sometimes he had to sprint to catch the ball. Sometimes he would bounce the ball. He continued this playful running until the end of his run. When he checked his watch he found he had run his fastest time ever on that particular course. He realized that since he was having fun, he didn't realize how hard he was running. His name was Ken Martin, America's fastest marathon runner that year (1989).

2. Distribute one tennis ball to each person.

3. Instruct participants to jog and play with the tennis ball on their run. Students may choose to dribble their ball, play catch with themselves or with a partner.

Suggestions:

- ❏ This activity works best on a hard surface.

- ❏ Debrief this warm-up with a discussion of how we tend to repeat activities that are enjoyable, so try to make fitness activities playful.

1.10 TOUCH

Grade Level: K-8, but most appropriate for K-3

Description: A quick warm-up for the beginning of class, especially when lots of equipment is out.

Objective: To touch as many objects in the room as possible in one minute (or other time period).

Equipment: Whatever equipment is to be used in the regular lesson

Directions:

1. Explain that in a 60-second time period, students are to attempt to touch as many objects as possible. This can include walls, doors, etc.

2. Mention any objects that you wish to be off limits (including yourself).

3. Repeat several times. Challenge participants to beat their best score.

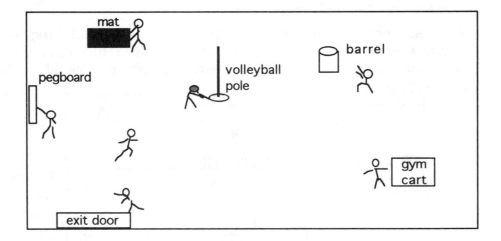

Suggestions:

❐ Allow objects to include people as well as things. Indicate whether the teacher is excluded or included in this. The activity then becomes a form of tag game.

❐ Stress quickness and trying to touch each object only once.

❐ If there is little or no equipment out, use the lines on the floor.

1.11 VOLLEYBALL SERVE RACE

Grade Level: 3-8

Description: Students receive cardio-vascular exercise and the experience of serving while under pressure. This warm-up is also a review of correct serving technique. It is a good way to make serving practice both active and competitive.

Objective: To serve, as quickly as possible, ten (or other number) serves across the net into the opposing court.

Equipment: A volleyball court with net; 1 ball per person

Directions:

1. Distribute one volleyball (or plastic volleyball) to each player.

2. Review correct serving procedure. Students may serve from anywhere on the back line.

3. Explain to students the task: to serve correctly into the proper court **ten** serves as quickly as possible.

4. Each student will retrieve his or her own ball, remembering to duck under the net if the ball is on the opposite side. Have students go to a winners' circle or similar area when they have completed the task.

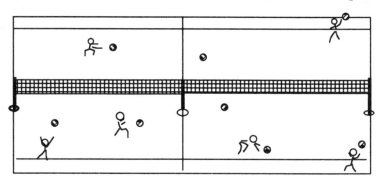

Suggestions:

❐ Repeat several times for a good workout and serve practice.

❐ This is best done on the honor system but, alternately, partners could be assigned to count for the server.

❐ Adjust serving line and height of net to suit the needs of the group.

RUNNING ACTIVITIES

Too often kids seem to fear running. Many may be frightened with shortness of breath. One reason for these fears may be that they have experienced too many timed runs. Running as hard as you can hurts, and most of us fear pain, at least to some extent.

Explain to kids the way adults run. If adults race at all, it's once every few weeks. And yes, that race hurts. But most runs are just training runs (refer to "Talk Test Run") and should not be that difficult; in fact, they can be very enjoyable. It's as true of kids as it is adults: we continue what we enjoy.

The focus of these running activities is to make running enjoyable. And shouldn't that be a goal of all physical education activities—to encourage lifetime participation by making them fun?

ACTIVITY INDICATOR

◯   Less active

◉   Active

●   Very active

Ⓢ   Strength

2.1 ADVENTURE RUN

Grade Level: K-6

Description: A great way to get kids hooked on the fun of running. This is an obstacle course running warm-up.

Objective: To negotiate the course (including obstacles) during the time period allowed.

Equipment: Use whatever obstacles are available naturally, but you can add equipment like tires, a pole suspended from two trees, etc.; traffic cones or lime

Directions: Mark the adventure run with lime or cones. Here is an example.

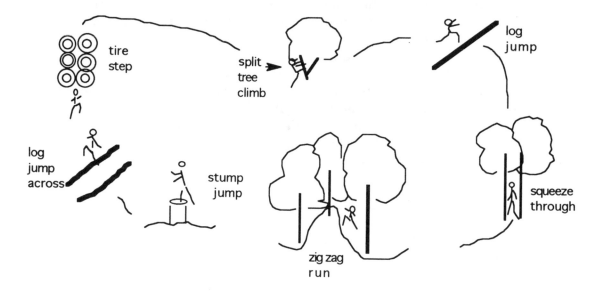

Suggestions: Kids love it when you lead such a run (the first lap anyway). Additionally, you will not need to mark the course if you show them the way.

2.2 CROSS COUNTRY RELAY

Grade Level: 3-8

Description: A competitive running event using the cross country course, but adding variety by using a relay format.

Objective: To complete the course as fast as possible as a group.

Equipment: Batons for each team, although hand tags work just as well; traffic cones (or natural markings)

Directions:

1. Divide the class into four-person teams (or other number of your choice).

2. Send one runner from each team to the four designated spots. Traffic cones are good markers, but so too are natural markings (the big tree, the backstop, the top of the hill, the sidewalk, etc.).

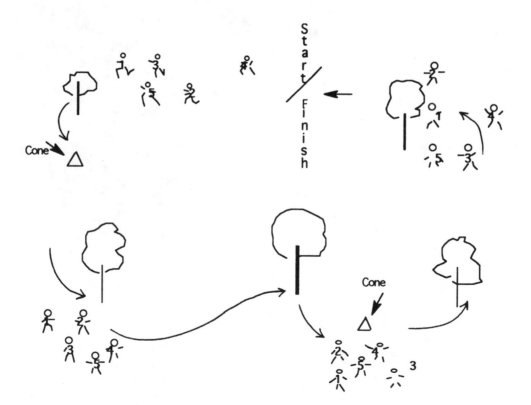

3. At starting signal, the first runner on each team runs to the next spot and tags off or hands a baton to the next runner on his or her team. Continue in like manner until the race is over.

Suggestions:

❐ All sections of the course do not have to be of equal length. One might be 200 yards; another, 300. In this case you might allow the teams to decide who runs the long section, the hilly part, etc.

❐ After the race is over, have students stay at their new markers. Following a short rest, start a second race.

2.3 ENDLESS RELAY

Grade Level: 1-8

Description: Run on an oval track; participants practice baton passing and interval training.

Objective: To run as fast as possible around the track and hand off the baton to your teammates.

Equipment: 1 baton for each 3-person team (sections of 3/4" PVC pipe make inexpensive batons); use different colored tape on batons to identify teams by color; traffic cones or lime

Description:

1. Mark the track using cones or lime.

2. Line up students in one line, shoulder to shoulder. Quickly count the number of students. Divide this number by 3 (i.e., $18/3 = 6$).

3. Students will count off by this number (1,2,3,4,5,6, 1,2,3,4,5,6, etc.).

4. Call all the #1's to stand in a line at the starting line.

5. Repeat step 4 for the #2's, #3's, etc.

6. Have the first and second persons in each line stay at the starting line while the third runner goes to the opposite side of the track as shown in the illustration.

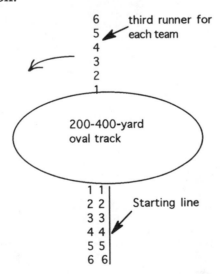

7. Each runner at the head of the line holds a baton.

8. On the starting signal the first runner from each team runs halfway around the track and hands off the baton to the next runner waiting there, who then runs the rest of the way around the track and hands off to the person waiting at the starting line. Since each runner waits where he or she handed off the baton, the relay goes on indefinitely.

Suggestions:

❐ Stop the event before kids begin to get too tired.

❐ Encourage waiting players to call out to their teammate runners so the incoming runner knows who to hand off the baton to.

2.4 "GUESS YOUR TIME" RUN

Grade Level: 3-8

Description: A different competitive running event, to be sure; one in which sense of pace is more important than speed.

Objective: To accurately predict your finish time for a running course.

Equipment: A small slip of paper for each participant; pencils

Directions:

1. This event is done *after* students have previously run a course for time.

2. Each participant writes on a slip of paper the time in which he or she expects to complete the running course. (This can be done before class.)

3. All participants run the course (with no watches allowed).

4. As each runner finishes, the teacher *quietly* calls out the time to each runner as he or she crosses the finish line.

5. Allow students time to calculate the time difference between their actual time and their predicted time. *The winners are those runners closest to their predictions.* In the example below, Mary would win over Jay.

Jay Smith	
Actual Time	4:35
Predicted time	4:20
Difference	:15

Mary Swift	
Predicted time	4:37
Actual Time	4:25
Difference	:12

Suggestions:

❏ Let kids do the calculations in small groups of three or four. They can recheck each other's math.

❏ It doesn't matter whether the student underestimates or overestimates his or her time. Simply subtract the lesser time from the greater. The result is the "difference" between actual and predicted time.

2.5 LOCATION RUN

Grade Level: K-8

Description: An active outside warm-up that also serves as a review of previously taught activities. A form of circuit training using review activities instead of exercises.

Objective: To run/jog to an area in order to work with the equipment located there.

Equipment: Whatever review equipment the teacher chooses

Directions:

1. Set out, before class, several boxes containing equipment that you want to review, such as Frisbees™, jump ropes, lacrosse, etc., at several locations around the grounds, within sight of the students.

2. Explain what is to be done at each station.

3. Divide students into groups (as many groups as stations—three or four work well).

4. Instruct students that they are to jog/run to the next location when the signal to change is given.

5. Disperse students to each station and allow them to begin. When the signal to change is given, students place the equipment back into the box and jog/run to the next area. This is repeated until all groups have been to all stations.

Suggestions:

❑ Timing is most important to this activity. Students should have enough time to get to the station and review a few skills, but keep it brief. About three to five minutes might be a good time period.

❑ Set out equipment several hundred yards apart so students are doing a form of interval training; vigorous running alternated with less active skill work.

❑ The teacher should be positioned at the activity requiring the most supervision.

2.6 MULTI-SCHOOL RUNNING EVENTS

Grade Level: 3-8

Description: A way to challenge young runners by providing them with the opportunity to take part in a higher level of competition. This is also a great way for your students to meet with students from other neighborhoods. These are cross country runs from ½ to 1½ miles in length (1 mile seems to be a good medium distance). It may, at first, appear to be a lot of work, but after putting on an event once, it is easier the following years.

Objective: To get together students from the various schools in your area to compete in cross country runs. NOTE: This is a voluntary program for both students and teachers.

Equipment: Cones or lime to mark the course; a stop watch; time check sheets (see Section 10, "Ready-to-Use Forms"); masking tape; finish boards; pennants or flags add a nice touch in a finish chute; a megaphone is also a big help

Directions:

1. Get permission from your supervisor and/or school principals to put on these events.

2. Have a meeting of interested teachers in your area to set up a schedule of events—two or more dates. At this meeting, designate locations for each event, time (after school), distance, etc. Send out a copy of this schedule to all schools in your area.

3. All teachers interested will then begin to inform their students of these events and to prepare students by doing cross country running as part of their regular classes. The in-class running does not have to be equal in distance to the after-school run. Experts say a normally active child can run one mile or more without any special training.

4. Before each event, send home permission slips to interested students, informing parents of the specifics of the event: time, place, etc. Without parental support, this program just can't work. Teachers cannot transports students. Include a tentative order of events (see the following example). Also see Section 10, "Ready-to-Use Forms," for sample letters.

3rd and 4th grade girls	4:00 p.m.
3rd and 4th grade boys	4:15 p.m.
5th grade girls	4:30 p.m.
5th grade boys	4:45 p.m.

5. The host teacher will prepare the course and act as race organizer. Use parents as volunteers or utilize the teachers from the various schools to assist (see below).

Jobs of Volunteers:

1. **Timer**—Calls out a time for each runner crossing the finish line.

2. **Scorer**—On a pre-made check sheet (see Diagram #1), puts a √ beside each time called out by the timer. There may be two or more √s at one time. See Section 10, "Ready-to-Use Forms" for actual forms.)

3. **Judge**—Stands at the finish line and makes decisions on close finishes.

4. **Finish chute mover**—Keeps runners moving through the finish chute.

5. **Tape puller**—*Each runner must have a piece of masking tape with his or her name and school written on it.* Students wear this tape on the front of their running clothes. The tape puller removes this tape and places it on a pre-made board (see Diagram #2). Boards can be made out of plywood, plastic sheets, plexiglass, etc. After the race, take the check-off sheet and add times onto the pieces of masking tape. In this way all runners can see their times and places shortly after the event.

6. **Optional**—If your school can afford it, award a participant's ribbon to each person at the end of the chute.

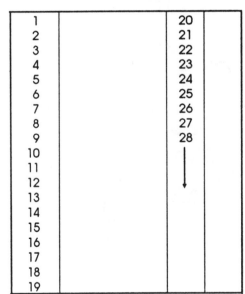

Diagram #1   Diagram #2

Suggestions:

☐ Do not be tempted to train your elementary students. The idea is to experience cross country running. Serious training should not begin until about ages 13-15. The ultimate goal is enjoyment of competition and running. And no runner likes to run hard every session, so many of the in-class runs should be untimed training runs.

☐ Mail results to each school competing but do not keep a team score; it should be an individual competition.

☐ Anyone can run regardless of ability—all that's needed is desire. Slower runners can enjoy racing, too!

☐ Try not to have any cross-over sections on your running course.

☐ If you have a small campus, consider two loops of a half mile course.

☐ Make the course interesting with turns, short hills, etc., not just loops around a soccer field.

☐ The course should have a relatively wide, straight starting area (50 yards or so before the first turn) and a straight, unobstructed finish area.

☐ Award ribbons to the top ten finishers and/or give a ribbon of participation to each runner.

2.7 MULTI-START RACES

Grade Level: 3-8

Description: An unusual running event in that everyone has an equal chance to win!

Objective: To be first across the finish line by being the most improved runner in the event.

Equipment: Forms; stopwatch

Directions:

1. This event is done after students have been timed over a running course. Record the times. These times will allow you to set up the multi-start race.

Times for first run on course:

John	4:20		Sue	3:52
Bill	4:11		Nora	3:58
Mary	4:15		Todd	4:56
Sarah	4:12		Tim	4:27
Tom	4:30		Lisa	4:05
Bob	5:00		Jeff	3:55
Terry	3:40			

2. Make up a *blank* form (no names yet) like the example shown in Form #1. Begin with the fastest time ever recorded on the course and end with the slowest anticipated time. (See Section 10 for the actual form.)

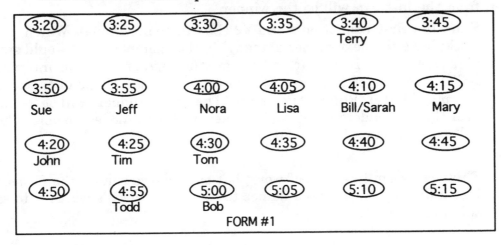

3. Put the students' names on Form #1 under the time that is *closest* to the time they ran in the first race. You may have many names under one time. That's okay.

4. Now place these names in reverse order (with slowest now being first) on Form #2. (Again, see Section 10 for the actual form.)

seconds

0	Bob	55	Lisa
5	Todd	1:00	Nora
10		1:05	Jeff
15		1:10	Sue
20		1:15	
25		1:20	Terry
30	Tom	1:25	
35	Tim	1:30	
40	John	1:35	
45	Mary		
50	Bill/Sarah		

order of starting ↓

FORM #2

5. To run the race, explain to students that the order of finish will be reversed and, if everyone runs to their potentials, they should all get to the finish together. So instead of starting together and finishing far apart, the reverse will be true. But the person who improves the most from the last run will be the winner.

6. Start the first runner on Form #2 (Bob in the example). Watch your clock; have the next runner(s) ready. In the example, Todd would start 5 seconds after Bob. Start others at the appropriate time intervals. NOTE: The faster runners will have lots of targets ahead of them and will play kind of "Running Pac-Man." The slower runners will be looking over their shoulders—they've likely never been in the lead before. They will be pushed on by the chasers.

Note:

❏ This may seem like a lot of work, but once you've run off the forms, it just takes transferring the names to the form. And it's worth it to see this unique race.

2.8 PURSUIT RELAY

Grade Level: 3-8

Description: An indoor or outdoor relay running event, with a few interesting variations. This activity develops quickness in oval running (as in track or diamond games) and is also a good way to teach the concepts of "clockwise" and "counterclockwise."

Objective: To catch the runner from the team ahead of you.

Equipment: 3 traffic cones and 3 Nerf™ footballs or other soft balls

Directions:

1. Set up three cones an equal distance apart in the available space. Leave a safety zone of two to three yards *behind* each cone.

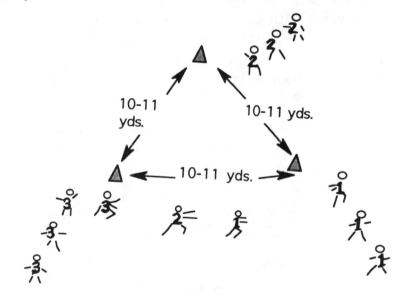

10-11 yds.   10-11 yds.   10-11 yds.

2. Divide the class into three teams. Each team lines up behind one of the three cones. The first person in each line is given a soft Nerf™ or other soft ball.

3. On the starting signal, the **first** person in each line will run **one** time around the three cones chasing the runner from the team ahead of him or her. The race is ended when a runner passes or tags (with the ball) the runner from the team ahead.

4. If no runner has caught the runner ahead by the end of the one lap, the runner will tag the next person on his or her respective team who takes up the chase. The race continues until someone is caught.

5. Start a new race with the next person in each line beginning the chase.

Suggestion:

❏ Make sure those waiting in line stay back away from the cones to allow room for the passing runners.

Variations:

❏ Give the chaser the option of *throwing* the ball at the runner ahead. He or she may still tag or pass, if desired. Of course, if the throw misses the runner, the chaser must chase down the ball and continue.

❏ Try the above variation with a soft Nerf™ football. NOTE: In both of these variations, the runner can pass the ball to the next runner on the team as long as both are on the same side of the triangle.

❏ If you have some soft pillows or some sort of well-padded club, play the same game with the winners being the first to bonk the runner ahead on the shoulder or back.

❏ As you start each contest, call out either "Clockwise" or "Counterclockwise." Participants will have to be alert and quickly decide in which direction to chase.

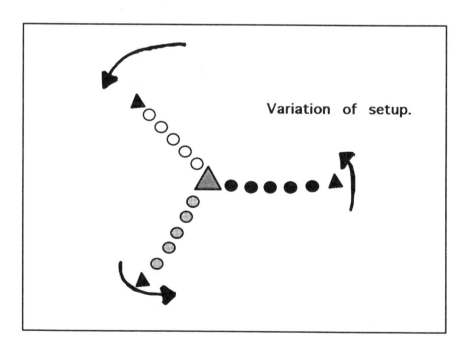

Variation of setup.

2.9 RUN A MILE +

Grade Level: 1-8

Description: A challenge for students—how many can run one mile without stopping? Speed doesn't matter in this run, so everyone can be a winner.

Objective: For students to attempt to run one mile without stopping or walking.

Equipment: Course marking

Directions:

1. Set up at least one jogging course. For variety you might have both a ¼-mile course around a soccer field and a ½-mile cross country. Students can then choose which course(s) they want to run to complete the mile. (A short discussion of fractions may be needed.)

2. Explain that in this event speed doesn't matter; students may go as slowly as they like—but if they have to stop or walk, the event is over.

3. Encourage students to go at the best pace for them. Suggest finding a running partner of the same speed to make the run more enjoyable.

4. Have a review activity (like a soccer game) for students to go to after they have finished their run and gotten a drink of water.

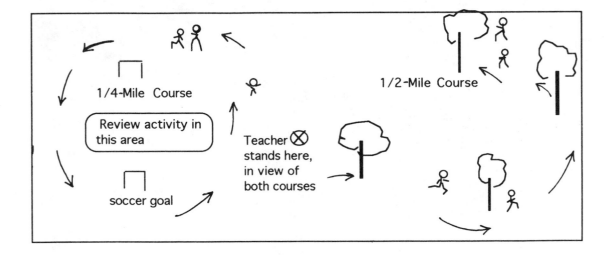

Suggestions:

❏ You might use this opportunity to explain the difference between running and walking. In walking both feet are on the ground at one time, whereas in running, both feet come off the ground at some point in the stride.

❏ Post names of all those students who complete the mile non-stop.

❏ For grades 3 and up, allow those specially motivated students to go farther (up to three miles). Record these names in a special section. NOTE: Many students claim the 3-mile run is easier than the ½-mile cross country timed run! They say they get into an easy cadence and there is no respiratory distress. And they enjoy jogging along while talking with their friends. They also get a great sense of accomplishment in completing a distance they once thought impossible.

2.10 SCOUT PACE RUN

Grade Level: K-8

Description: A running/walking event that teaches students a way to cover long distances comfortably.

Objective: To cover a given distance with a combination of running and walking.

Equipment: A running/walking course

Directions:

1. Ask students to find a partner of nearly equal running ability for this event.

2. Explain the Boy Scout method of covering long distances; that is, alternating between running and walking.

3. As the event starts, the first partner will count 50 running steps (counting each time the right foot strikes the ground). At the end of this count of 50 running steps, both partners begin walking with the second partner counting 50 walking steps. Partners alternate in this way throughout the course.

4. This is not a race, just a way of demonstrating how easy it is to travel a long distance using this method.

Suggestions:

❏ Do as a warm-up activity or part of a cross country unit.

❏ Discuss the reaction of students to this run/walk. Was it easy, hard, fun, etc.?

2.11 SOCIAL RUN

Grade Level: K-8

Description: A run that describes the social aspect of working out.

Objective: To run with friends in an enjoyable way.

Equipment: Running area

Directions:

1. Explain the process that adults would follow if getting together to run with friends. They would discuss and agree upon where to run, what time, how far, and at what pace.

2. Explain that students may join together in groups of two or more to discuss where in the area they would like to run. The main rule in social running is that *the group always matches its pace to the slowest runner in the group.*

3. Allow an appropriate time for running. Walking breaks are allowed, just as adults might do.

4. Regroup after the run to discuss the enjoyment of social running, the health benefits, any problems that arose, and the need to keep the concept of fun in most of our training.

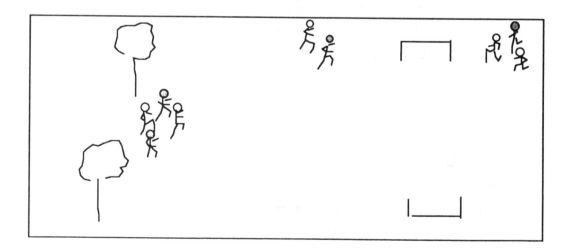

2.12 TALK TEST RUN

Grade Level: K-8

Description: A warm-up run that teaches correct aerobic effort.

Objective: To run at a pace that allows for a moderate amount of talking with friends.

Equipment: Running area

Directions:

1. Explain that in this running activity you *want students to talk,* but not in long paragraphs or in short gasps. If the effort is right, participants should be able to talk in short phrases and sentences; in other words, they should be just slightly out of breath.

2. Describe the general area of the run, or mark off the running area.

3. Allow students to group themselves in small groups or pairs.

Suggestion:

☐ For this event to work best, runners should be of approximately equal running ability. An easy way to group students in this way is to say "Choose one or two partners with whom you are equal in running ability."

2.13 THROW 'N GO

Grade Level: Suitable for K-8, but most appropriate for K-3

Desription: An activity that combines skill work and aerobic conditioning.

Objective: To work on various sports skills in a way that develops cardiovascular fitness.

Equipment: 1 soccer ball, Frisbee™, lacrosse stick and ball, or tennis ball, etc., for each person participating; mark a starting line; target

Directions:

1. Line up participants (about eight to ten at a time) on the starting line with whatever equipment you are using in the lesson.

2. Point out the target (fence, backstop, wall) that players are racing toward. About 100-200 yards away is a good distance.

3. Explain that to win the race, they must be the first to hit the distant target with their chosen equipment and get back across the starting line. The main rule of the contest: *Players may not run with the throwing or kicking implement*—they run to it, throw or kick, and repeat.

Suggestions:

❐ Since this is a very active racing event, it is suggested that the class be divided into smaller groups. Have those not participating stand off to the side—resting for their turn. Groups will not have to wait more than a few minutes before it is their turn to participate.

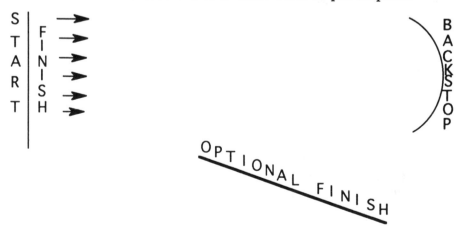

Variation: Generally when racing toward a large target, kids spread out enough that those coming back do not interfere with those still going toward the target. But, if you like, make it a triangular course so that racers do not run back into outgoing students (as in the above optional finish). Have watching students call off finishers' places as their ball crosses the line.

2.14 WHISTLE PACE RUN

Grade Level: 1-8

Description: A run that teaches even pace. You will have many winners in this event.

Objective: To finish the running course in exactly the time established by the teacher.

Equipment: An approximately ¼-mile flat running area; whistle; cones or other markers to divide the course into four equal sections as shown in the illustration.

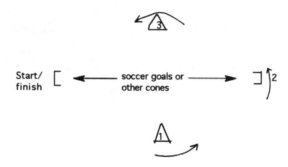

Directions:

1. Explain to students that it will take about 100 seconds to run this course. NOTE: Adjust the time for different ability groups and/or different distances. The time should be reachable for all students.

2. The winner(s) of this run are those who finish *within three seconds* of the stated time.

3. To assist runners, the teacher will blow a whistle every 25 seconds after the start. This allows runners who arrive at the first cone before 25 seconds to slow their pace and runners who arrive after 25 seconds to pick up their pace.

Suggestions:

❑ For the first time, students will probably race the course. Just ignore these runners and announce as winners all those runners who finish within three seconds of the established time.

❑ Repeat a few times and all runners will probably finish exactly on time.

Section **3**

ACTIVE GAMES

Active games are the most enjoyable way to increase children's fitness levels. "Stop-and-start" is the natural play of children. Students can self-pace by alternately running and stopping or slowing as they play many of these active games. The following are some additional suggestions when including aerobic games and activities in your program.

Teaching Hints for Aerobic Games and Activities

1. Eliminate elimination. Provide alternate activities for those not actively participating. Or provide a quick return to the action if the game is of an elimination type.

2. Try to have games last at least five minutes before changing teams or stopping play.

3. Increase the size of the field. Moving goals farther apart encourages more running.

4. Keep to a minimum pauses in the game for penalties, out of bounds, directions, etc.

5. Add more balls to the game to increase the amount of movement and skill use.

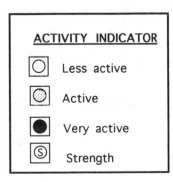

3.1 COLOR TAG

Grade Level: K-8

Description: A very fast tag game for indoor or outdoor play.

Equipment 3 different colored jerseys; one jersey for each player; stopwatch

Directions:

1. Divide class into three teams. Each team wears a different colored jersey, for example, red, yellow, and blue.

2. The teacher calls out, "Ready, set, **Red!**" The teacher starts a stop watch. The red team then attempts to tag all of the blue and yellow teams' players.

3. Players sit down when tagged or go to a side area to sit down.

4. When all the blue and yellow players have been tagged, the teacher stops the clock.

5. Announce the time to the class.

6. Repeat steps 2-5 for blue and yellow teams.

7. Compare times of the teams.

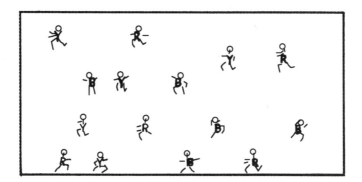

Suggestion:

❐ This game is very strenuous. Follow it with something less active.

3.2 FITNESS TAG

Grade Level: K-8

Description: A fast action warm-up game that has as many variations as you have exercises. Both strength and aerobic conditioning are combined in this one. Play indoor or outdoor.

Objective: For selected players to tag runners. The runners' goal is to avoid being tagged.

Equipment: 4 different colored scrimmage vests

Directions:

1. Select four students to be taggers. Each will wear a different-colored vest.

2. When these four people tag someone else in the game, the person tagged must perform an exercise before resuming play. Examples:

   If tagged by the red vest person—do five push-ups.

   If tagged by the blue vest person—do five sit-ups.

   If tagged by the green vest person—do ten jumping jacks.

   If tagged by the yellow vest person—do five toe touches.

   Exercises can be done at the point of being tagged or off in a separate area.

Suggestions:

❑ The game can be played with more or fewer taggers.

❑ Pick new taggers for each game—this also gives the runners a slight "breather" while shirts are being exchanged.

❑ Change exercises as you like.

❑ You might want the taggers to call out the exercise when they tag someone.

3.3 FLAG FOOTBALL TAG

Grade Level: 3-8

Description: A tag game for the whole class that teaches open field running with a football.

Objective: For the defense to pull the flags of ball carriers and for the offense to score a touchdown by running across the goal line with both flags still on their belts and the football in their hands.

Equipment: 1 flag football belt (with two flags of the same color) for each player; enough footballs for half the class; cones or lime

Directions:

1. Mark the field with lime or cones as shown.

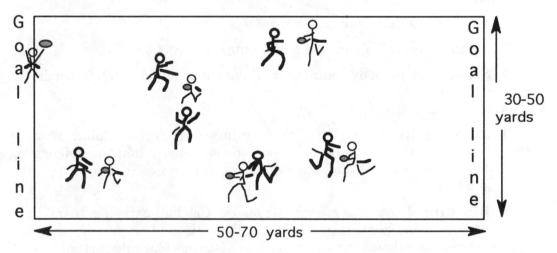

2. Divide the class into two groups. Distribute different-colored flag football belt sets to each player.

3. Demonstrate flag-pulling **rules:**
   a. No player may hold another in an attempt to remove their flags.
   b. Players may not hold their flags to keep others from pulling them off.
   c. Pulling one or both flags prohibits a runner from scoring.
   d. No defensive player may dive at a ball carrier.

4. One group (red flags) stands on a goal line. Each team member has a football.

5. The other team (yellow flags) stands in the middle of the field.

6. Explain that each red team member will attempt to run across the opposing team's goal line carrying his or her football and still wearing both flags.

7. Yellow team members will attempt to stop as many red players as possible by removing one or both flags from the red players' belts. They should drop flags on the ground when pulled.

8. If a red player's flag is pulled, he or she drops the football, picks up his or her flag, and walks to the goal line. *Only the ball carriers' flags are pulled.*

9. All ball carriers successfully reaching the goal line hold up their footballs signifying their score. Victory dance is optional!

10. Offense and defense switch roles after each run.

Suggestions:

❏ Use soft footballs for greatest safety.

❏ Discuss deceptive running and change of direction.

❏ Stress that no body contact other than flag pulling should occur.

Variation:

❏ **Strategy Run:** Have the ball-carrying team devise a plan. *Example:* Send two runners as decoys down one sideline. When the defense goes after these two players, the remaining runners escape down the other sideline.

❏ **Blocking Run:** Have each player on the ball-carrying team find a partner. One partner hikes the ball to his or her partner who runs behind the hiker, who acts as a shield. Discuss blocking (actually shielding since there is no body contact). The shielder should run in front of the ball carrier. As a defensive player goes around the shielder to get to the ball carrier, the ball carrier goes around the other side of the shielder.

3.4 FLAG TAG

Grade Level: K-4

Description: A game that requires quick hands, quick eyes, and lots of stamina. It can be played indoor or outdoor.

Objective: To eliminate other players by pulling out their flags.

Equipment: 1 flag for each player (possible flags include: regular jerseys, flag-football flags, or strips of cloth 1½-2 feet long)

Directions:

1. Play on a field equal to about half of a regular soccer field.

2. Distribute one flag to each player. Instruct players to tuck the end of the flag into the **back** of their waistbands. About one foot of flag should hang down in the back.

3. Explain the **rules:**
   a. A player cannot hold another player when pulling out a flag. Some body contact is inevitable, however.
   b. A player may not hold his or her flag to keep it from being pulled.
   c. When a flag is pulled out, it is dropped onto the floor or ground. The player who lost it carries the flag to the sideline and awaits the next game.

4. Explain that the last player (or last two or three if you choose) is the winner. Games go fast, especially in a smaller area like a gym.

Variations:

❐ Play team against team. Divide the group into two equal teams; use different colored flags for each team. In this version, teammates may work together to capture the flag of an opposing player. Start teams at opposite ends of the field.

❐ When playing Team Flag Tag, have the losing team invite one player from the winning team to join their team. This does three things: (1) the losing team is more likely to win the next game; (2) the person selected feels like a hero; and (3) no team can finish the game claiming victory because the teams become jumbled. When using this strategy, alternate between selecting girls and boys, and have a rule that no player can be picked twice.

3.5 MONSTER FROM MARS

Grade Level: K-3

Description: A variation of an old favorite tag game that teaches young children recognition of colors, designs, and patterns. It's great for teaching the vocabulary associated with these concepts. This can be played indoor or outdoor.

Objective: To be the first selected person to tag the Monster.

Equipment: None

Directions:

1. Have all students stand on one line at the end of the gym, or a similar line outside.
2. Select one player to be the Monster. This player stands out in front of the other players and faces them.
3. The group chants, "Monster from Mars, Monster from Mars, may we chase you to the stars?" The Monster responds, "Yes, you may, if you are wearing . . ." The Monster then calls out a color. All those students with the designated color on their clothing begin chasing the Monster. The first player to tag the Monster becomes the new Monster.

Variation:

❏ Expand the selection of reponses by the Monster to include "stripes," "black shoes," "glasses," "short sleeves," "ribbons in your hair," "a gold fish at home," etc. Encourage creative responses.

Suggestion:

❏ Select **two** Monsters. These two "huddle" together and choose one response to give the chasers. This allows more students to have a chance at being the Monster.

3.6 OCTOPUS TAG

Grade Level: K-6

Description: Easy to set up and fun to play, with lots of running. This can be played indoor or outdoor, but it's best played on grass.

Objective: To tag players as they run across the area.

Equipment: Field markings

Directions:

1. Set up the field of play, approximately 30 yards wide and 40 yards long.

2. Have all students stand on one end line.

3. Select one (or two) players as the "Octopus" (or "Octopi") to stand in the center of the playing field.

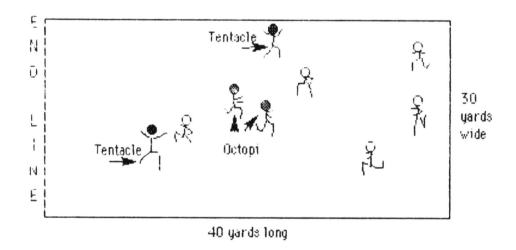

4. Explain that the remaining players are Fish and are to attempt to swim (run) across the sea (playing area).

5. The Octopi will run and try to tag as many Fish as possible. When tagged a Fish becomes a Tentacle of an Octopus and must keep one foot anchored in the stop where he was tagged.

6. Fish that successfully run to the other side of the playing area stop, and then, on the next starting signal from the teacher, run back across the area.

7. This continues until all Fish have been turned into Tentacles.

Suggestion:

❑ Remind Tentacles that they must keep one foot anchored. They may pivot.

3.7 PAC-MAN

Grade Level: K-3

Description: A modernized version of a familiar tag game, this is a large group activity for the gym or field. Very active!

Objectives: (1) The *Pac-Men* try to eliminate the Ghosts and Power Pellets by pulling out their shirts or flags. (2) The *Power Pellets* attempt to "re-energize" eliminated Ghosts to get them back into the game. (3) The *Ghosts* try to avoid getting caught.

Equipment:

1. 5-6 Pac-Man shirts. I use yellow pinnies with the Pac-Man logo drawn on the front and back. The players who wear these shirts are designated as Pac-Men. If the group is large, use more shirts. Also, enlarge playing area to suit the size of the class. In a small area the ghosts are easily eliminated.

2. Two different colored shirts (not yellow). The players who wear these shirts are designated as the Power Pellets.

3. Pieces of cloth, regular pinnies, or one flag-football belt flag for each player in the class *except* the Pac-Men. These players (except the two Power Pellets) are designated as Ghosts.

Directions:

1. All players, except the Pac-Men, tuck a shirt or flag into the back of their waistbands so that about one foot of material hangs down in back.

Shirts or cloth should not be wrapped around belts—they must be easily pulled out.

2. Select two Power Pellets who wear their special shirts in addition to the material tucked in back.

3. Select five to six players to wear the special Pac-Men shirts.

4. Explain the other **rules:**

    a. If eliminated, a Ghost sits down and remains out until a Power Pellet taps him or her on the head, thereby re-energizing and allowing the Ghost back into the game.

    b. The Pac-Men also can try to eliminate the two Power Pellets by pulling out their shirts. However, one Power Pellet can re-energize the other. If all Ghosts and Power Pellets are eliminated, the game is over.

    c. No player may hold another player when pulling out a shirt, and may not hold onto his or her own shirt to keep it from being pulled.

Suggestion:

❏ Periodically switch Pac-Men, Ghosts, and Power Pellets.

Variation:

❏ With grades 2 and 3, you might allow any two "active" Ghosts to also re-energize a "downed" Ghost by joining hands around the "downed" Ghost to create a life giving "Force Field," thus enabling the Ghost a return to active play.

3.8 TREE TAG

Grade Level: K-4

Description: An aerobic warm-up game for younger students that teaches the concept of being "safe" on base. The whole class plays at once.

Objective: For the selected three to four taggers to tag players who are not safely on base (touching a tree).

Equipment: 3-4 soft Nerf™ balls or other visible object for tagging (so players can see who is "It"); trees in a safe area that doesn't have many obstacles (roots, limbs, etc.)

Directions:

1. Explain the **rules:**
   a. If tagged with the ball, the person tagged becomes "It."
   b. No "tag backs"—you can't tag the person who has just tagged you.
   c. If a person is touching a tree, he or she cannot be tagged.
   d. Only one player at a tree. If a second player comes to that tree, the first person must leave.

2. Explain boundaries so that the game is contained somewhat.

3. Give three or four students one Nerf™ ball each. They will start the game as taggers.

Suggestions:

❑ Encourage taggers to change directions—not just chase one player.

❑ For grades 2 and 3, allow throwing the Nerf™ ball to get a player out.

❑ No trees? Use bases instead. Just lay out six or so bases on the ground, floor, or hard court area. Game is played the same.

❑ Or try tube or hoop tag. Place hula hoops or inner tubes on the ground.

3.9 AEROBIC FRISBEE™

Grade Level: 3-8

Description: An outdoor team Frisbee™ game.

Objective: To score a traditional touchdown catch, received in the end zone.

Equipment: 1 Frisbee™ per game (regular, Aerobie, or soft Frisbee™—"Woosh Ring"); if it's windy, a deck tennis ring also works; scrimmage vests for one or both teams

Directions:

1. Set up field as shown. Two games can be played across a regular soccer field; just provide a safety zone (of about five yards) between the two games using cones or other markers for this.

2. Provide jerseys for one or both teams.

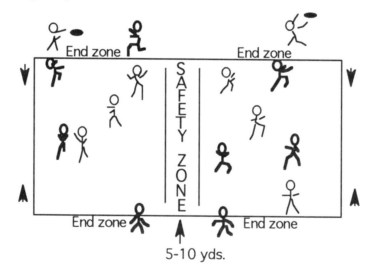

3. Explain the **rules:**
   a. Unlimited throwing and catching of the Frisbee™.
   b. No player may run while in possession of the Frisbee™. Other players may travel anywhere on the field.
   c. A team maintains possession of the Frisbee™ until a pass is intercepted by the opposing team, or a score is made.

d. The *thrower may not be guarded,* but all others may.

e. If the Frisbee™ lands on the ground, the first player who touches it gets a free throw. This avoids fighting over the Frisbee™.

Suggestion:

❐ Encourage players to move into open areas to receive passes.

3.10 BOUNCE BALL

Grade Level: 3-8 (with modified game for grades 1-2)

Description: An extremely simple-to-play indoor game (or outdoor on a hardcourt about 25 yards wide) that can have complex strategies. This game employs deceptive throwing and guarding skills.

Objective: To hit the opponent's wall with a bounced or rolled throw and to guard your wall against scores by the opponent.

Equipment: 3-5 red playground balls (6"-7") or some of the new low impact balls; start the game with 3 balls for a class of 25, 2 balls if group is fewer than 15 participants

Directions:

1. Divide group in half. Ask them to stand against the back wall. If the whole class is playing at once, play the game lengthwise in the gym, with the two teams separated by a center line as shown.

2. Explain the **rules:**
   a. The important rule is, *"The ball must touch the floor before hitting the opponent's back wall."* It may bounce off the side walls.
   b. The ball may be bounced over defenders.

c. The ball may be lobbed over defenders—as long as it touches the floor before hitting the wall.

d. Defenders may guard from anywhere on their half of the court.

Suggestions:

❑ Assign one student at each back wall as a counter or just play the game for fun and action.

❑ Adjust number of balls so that scoring is not too easy or too hard.

❑ For grades 1 and 2, play two games simultaneously across the gym, using folded mats to divide gym in half.

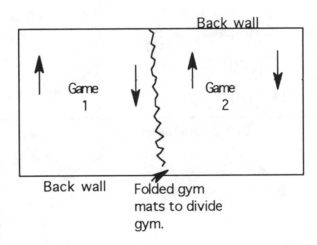

3.11 FIELD BALL

Grade Level: 3-8

Description: A modification of "Keepaway" that has two ways to score. A good game to teach deceptive passing.

Objective: To score points (one point for a pass that is caught in the scoring area; three points for a run across the goal line).

Equipment: 8 cones to mark the field; a small 5"-7" red playground ball or soft football; jerseys to distinguish teams

Directions:

1. Set up the field as shown:

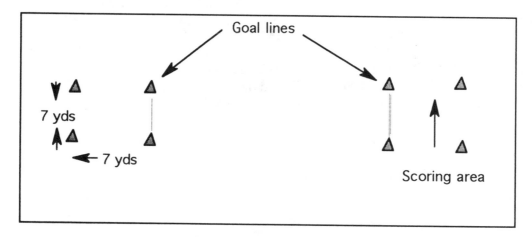

2. Distribute jerseys to one or both teams.
3. Each team selects a goalie.
4. Explain the **rules:**
   a. Players cannot score after being tagged.
   b. If tagged while carrying the ball, a player has three seconds to pass the ball.
   c. If a player is tagged while attempting to run across the goal line, a free throw is awarded to the opposing team at the goal line.
   d. After a score, play is started with a free throw by the goalie of the scored-upon team.

e. Players may run anywhere on the field.

5. **Scoring:** One point is scored if a pass is caught in the scoring area (marked by the four cones). Three points are scored if a player runs across the goal line without being tagged.

Suggestion:

❒ This game uses "Keepaway" rules, but with optional scoring. Encourage deception: faked throws, followed by a run across the goal line, and faked runs, followed by throws into the scoring area.

3.12 GHOST BUSTERS

Grade Level: K-8

Description: An indoor holiday game involving target throwing and guarding.

Objective: To remain in the game by protecting one's own ghost and to eliminate other players by knocking over their ghosts.

Equipment: Each player will need a large, clean, plastic milk container or bleach bottle. (Allow students to decorate bottles with ghost pictures using magic markers.) The bottles are the "ghosts." Plastic or wooden bowling pins also work in this game. Each player will need one soft, easy-to-throw ball. Sock balls work well (see Sock Balls in Section 7, "Things to Make") or any type of soft plastic or Nerf™ ball.

Directions:

1. Distribute one bottle and one ball to each player.

2. Each player places a bottle at his or her feet and holds a ball in his or her hand. Ghosts are not allowed to be placed against a wall.

3. Explain the **rules:**

   a. Players attempt to knock over other ghosts with a thrown ball while protecting their own.

   b. Players may guard their ghost with hands or feet, but may not touch any ghost.

c. Players must remain standing—no squatting or crouching.

d. When a player's ghost is knocked down (by another player or by herself or himself accidentally), that player goes to the Repair Shop (this can be a stage or side area) to wait for a new game. Use a folded mat to protect players who are out from being accidentally hit by thrown balls.

e. Players must be aware of the position of their ghosts at all times! In this way they will know whether they are in or out.

Suggestions:

❐ This can be an elimination game as explained above—last ghost remaining wins.

❐ However, for more action, send eliminated players out in order. When a designated number of players is out (say, seven), begin sending players back into the game—first out, first to come back in.

❐ Try a "get even" game. When out, a player stays out until the player who got him or her out is eliminated. If a player doesn't know who hit his or her ghost or the player knocked over his or her own ghost, he or she may just watch any player and come in when that player is eliminated.

❐ The most exciting time to play this game is during Halloween, using *Ghostbusters* music in the background.

3.13 HOOP BASKETBALL

Grade Level: 3-8

Description: A lead-up game that helps students with positioning on the basketball court. It also allows the team on offense more time to set up and make passes without too much defensive pressure.

Objective: To enable young students to be successful in the game of basketball.

Equipment: For each game—1 basketball, 2 baskets, and 4-5 hoops placed in front of each basket (8-10 hoops in all)

Directions:

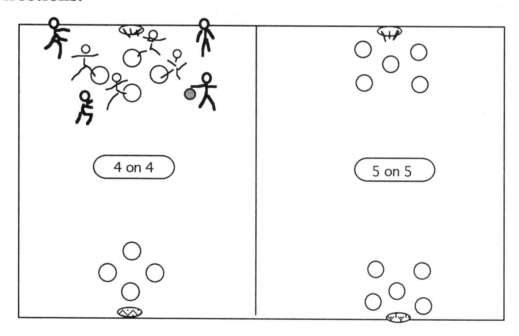

1. Set up hoops in front of baskets as shown.

2. Divide class into teams of four or five each.

3. Explain the **rules:**

   a. When on *defense,* players must keep one foot inside a hoop. They may steal a pass and get rebounds, but they may not steal a *dribbled* ball or take away a held ball.

b. The team on *offense* must complete two passes before taking their first shot. They may get their own rebound and continue shooting.

c. When the team on defense gets the ball, they must allow the other team a few seconds to get back into their defense positions at the other basket. There is *no press or fast break*.

4. Play two or more games across your gym. Play 4-on-4 or 5-on-5.

Suggestions:

❏ As long as players keep one foot inside the hoop, they may move around by pivoting—but they cannot move the hoop.

❏ If the hoops get knocked out of position too much, realign between games.

3.14 KEEPAWAY

Grade Level: 3-8

Description: This game is fun, very active, and teaches many of the valuable skills needed in such field games as basketball, lacrosse, football, and soccer. It is a throwing, catching, dodging, guarding game played outside on grass or hard-top court.

Objective: To score a point by running across your opponent's goal line without being tagged, or by successfully passing the ball across the goal line to a teammate.

Equipment: Cones or lime to mark the field; jerseys to distinguish teams; a ball that can be thrown with one hand and is easy to catch (I like the soft footballs with leather cover or a large sock ball)

Directions:

1. Mark the field according to the size of the group; set up as shown for eight players per team. Enlarge the field for larger groups.

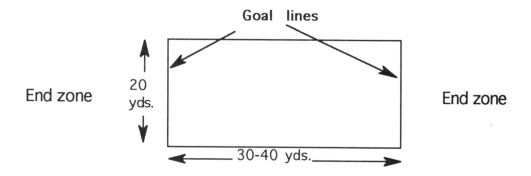

2. One team (or both) will need colored jerseys.

3. Many times the best games are those with the simplest rules. The basic rules of "Keepaway" are used in many field-type games included in this book, thus simplifying instruction for teacher and students. Explain the **rules** of the game:

   a. Players may move anywhere on the field or in the end zone.

   b. If tagged while carrying the ball, a player has three seconds to pass the ball.

c. Players cannot score after being tagged. They must pass off.

d. If a player is tagged while attempting to run across the goal line, a free throw is awarded to the opposing team at the goal line.

e. After a score, the opposing team restarts play with a free throw from the goal line.

f. Any penalty (holding ball beyond three seconds, etc.) and any out-of-bounds play results in a free throw for the opposing team.

4. Play is started with each team on its goal line. A throw or kick to the opposing team starts play.

Suggestions:

❏ Encourage passing to "open" players.

❏ Have a less vigorous activity for one-third of the class while the two teams play; then rotate teams so all get a break time.

3.15 LACROSSE

Grade Level: 3-8

Description: A safe version of lacrosse that's active and playable by young children with little lacrosse experience. It can be played on grass or on a hard-top court.

Objective: To score goals against the opposing team as in regular lacrosse but with a few rule modifications.

Equipment: 10 STX soft lacrosse sticks (5 of each color); two goals; use either a tennis ball or soft STX ball

Directions:

1. Mark the five yellow STX sticks with colored tape as follows:
   two sticks with a strip of black tape—for attack players
   two sticks with a strip of yellow tape—for the defensive players
   one stick with a strip of red tape—for the midfield player
   Mark the five green sticks likewise. Sticks are colored so players can know their position on the court and the teacher can quickly check the location of players.

2. Set up the field.

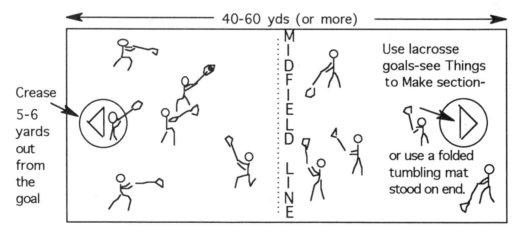

3. Explain the **rules** to players:
   a. No stick checking (hitting someone's stick in an effort to knock the ball out).

b. No player can go inside the crease except the goalie.

c. Two passes must be made before a shot can be made at goal. Any caught ball (rolling, bouncing, etc.) counts as a pass.

d. No player may cross the midfield line except the two midfielders. Other players will pass across the midfield line to their teammates.

e. Actual boundaries are not needed. They tend to slow the game.

f. A face off (see "Face Off Drill") is done to start the game and after each score. Alternately, the scored-upon goalie may start play.

g. Goalies must wear chest protection and mask. Softball equipment will serve this purpose.

Suggestions:

❏ Encourage players on defense to hold their sticks in front of their faces when defending. This gives them added protection from a shot being made toward them.

❏ Periodically switch offense and defense players.

3.16 LACROSSE—SMALL FIELD

Grade Level: 3-8

Description: A lacrosse game designed for a small field area or in the gym.

Objective: To score goals as in regular lacrosse.

Equipment: 2 lacrosse goals or other goals; 10 soft lacrosse sticks (5 of each color); one soft lacrosse ball or tennis ball; protective gear (chest protector and some sort of mask) makes the game safer

Directions:

1. Set up the goals as shown:

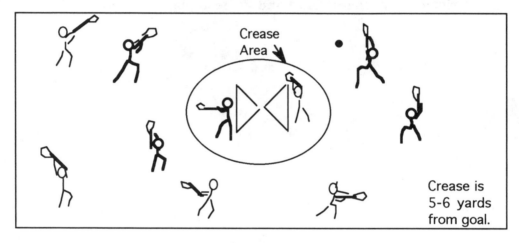

2. Explain the **rules** of the game:
   a. No checking (hitting of sticks) allowed.
   b. A loose ball may be fought for, but no pushing or other body contact.
   c. No player may go into the crease area, except the two goalies.
   d. After a score, the opposing goalie starts play with a free throw.

Suggestions:

❐ Try a two-pass rule. The ball must be passed twice before a shot can be made on goal.

❐ Players will have to be careful of shot selection because a missed shot will usually end up in front of the shooter's own goal!

3.17 NON-STOP BASKETBALL

Grade Level: 3-8

Description: The speediest basketball game ever; no stopping (except to gasp for air!)

Objective: To score points as in regular basketball, but with the emphasis on a great cardio-vascular workout rather than skill development.

Equipment: 1 basketball; 2 baskets; jerseys for one or both teams.

Directions:

1. Provide jerseys for one or both teams (five to eight players per team).
2. Explain the **rules** of the game:
   a. No out of bounds or time-outs.
   b. No penalties except those assessed by the teacher/leader. Do not stop the game for double dribbling, traveling, etc. The better players will naturally use correct basketball skills and the less skilled will do the best they can without the anxiety of penalties.

Suggestions:

❑ Stress fast-break play, lots of shots and quick passes, less dribbling.

❑ Assess penalties only to a player blatantly fouling or breaking rules.

❑ The emphasis is on action, not scoring.

3.18 NO-SWIPE BASKETBALL

Grade Level: 3-8

Description: A basketball game that enables less skilled players to handle the ball without pressure. This game is not meant for the highly skilled player, but for beginners who want to enjoy basketball without needing a referee to call fouls. Players of this age are usually much better at stealing a dribble than controlling a dribble.

Objective: To score points as in regular basketball.

Equipment: Regular or modified basketball equipment

Directions:

1. Play either half-court or full-court games.

2. Explain the special **rules** of this modified game:
   a. Regular basketball rules except that players cannot steal a ball from the dribbler.
   b. If the dribbler loses control of his or her dribble or the ball is passed, any opposing player may intercept.

Suggestions:

❐ Explain to students the purpose of this modified game. It's impossible for a teacher to referee more than one game, so this modification eliminates the need for officials and keeps play safe.

❐ This game works best with small groups (like three against three). This is a good time to also teach the rules of half-court basketball using a clear line.

3.19 POSTBALL

Grade Level: 4-8 (with variations for grades 1-3)

Description: This variation of a great old game can be played indoor or outdoor. I like the inside game because play is more continuous. This is a team game with "Keepaway" strategies and an interesting way of scoring.

Objective: To knock down the opposing team's bottle from the post.

Equipment: 2 volleyball standards or homemade posts (about 8-10 feet high); 2 large strong plastic bottles; a 6"-7" red playground ball; scrimmage vests for one or both teams

Directions:

1. Make postball and bottle set-up as shown:

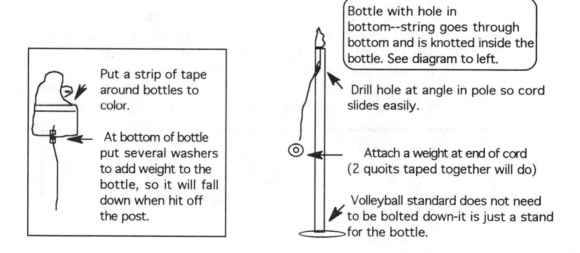

Put a strip of tape around bottles to color.

At bottom of bottle put several washers to add weight to the bottle, so it will fall down when hit off the post.

Bottle with hole in bottom--string goes through bottom and is knotted inside the bottle. See diagram to left.

Drill hole at angle in pole so cord slides easily.

Attach a weight at end of cord (2 quoits taped together will do)

Volleyball standard does not need to be bolted down-it is just a stand for the bottle.

2. Mark a circle (about 20 feet across) around posts.

3. Divide the class into teams of six or eight (depending on the size of the gym).

4. Provide scrimmage vests for one or both of the playing teams.

5. Explain the **"Keepaway" rules:**

   a. If tagged while carrying the ball, a player has three seconds to pass.

b. Players cannot score after being tagged.

c. Players cannot score from inside the circle.

6. A point is scored when a bottle is knocked off the pole. If the bottle is touched but doesn't fall, there is no score.

7. To get the bottle back on top of the pole, simply grab the weighted end of the string and pull so the bottle pops back up.

8. After a score, the bottle is set up and play starts immediately with a free throw from the circle by the just scored-upon team.

Suggestion:

❐ Don't worry about players going into the circle area; they can't possibly guard a bottle ten feet high. They will be much more effective guarding further away from the circle.

Variations:

❐ In grade 3 I use *two* 6"-7" red balls. Rules are the same. The first bottle to fall scores a point. As third graders get better at passing and positioning, etc., play with one ball.

❐ For grades 1 and 2, divide whole class into two teams (three if you have three postball standards). Again mark a circle around the posts. Have five to ten sock balls on the floor (experiment with number of balls). To play the game, use the same rules: players still can't score from inside the circle and can't score after being tagged by an opposing player. The team that keeps its bottle up longer wins the point.

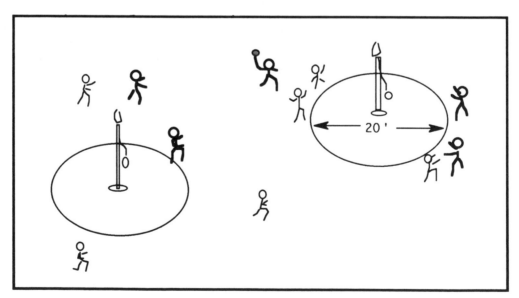

3.20 SCOOTER BASKETBALL

Grade Level: K-6

Description: A basketball game for small areas like the cafeteria, recreation room, or half the gym. This game necessitates good passing, since you can't travel with the ball in your possession. A definite favorite of kids!

Objective: To score points by throwing the ball into the trash barrel.

Equipment: 12-16 gym scooters; 1 Nerf™ soccer or Nerf™ basketball; 2 trash barrels; markers for the 2 crease areas

Directions:

1. Set up the field of play as shown:

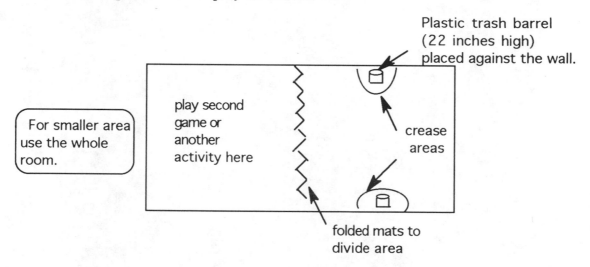

Plastic trash barrel (22 inches high) placed against the wall.

For smaller area use the whole room.

play second game or another activity here

crease areas

folded mats to divide area

2. Use cones or other markers to designate the crease areas. Adjust distance of crease circle area as needed, but start with 5-6 feet from the barrel.

3. If you have enough scooters, play two games; otherwise, have a different activity on the other half of the gym. NOTE: To divide the gym, try using folded gym mats—just stand them up on their sides (with a slight folding) to provide a safe, high barrier.

4. Explain the **rules**:

   a. All players must remain *seated* on their scooters at all times.

b. If a player has possession of the ball and falls off the scooter, it is a free pass for the nearest opposing player; likewise, if a player falls off the scooter while reaching for the ball.

c. Players may not travel on the scooter when in possession of the ball.

d. Players may shoot at the basket from anywhere outside the crease.

e. No one may go into the crease except to retrieve a loose ball on the floor.

3.21 SCOOTER TEAM HANDBALL

Grade Level: 1-6

Description: An active team game for small areas such as cafeterias, or half of a gymnasium. This game encourages team play and passing since players cannot travel when in possession of the ball.

Objective: To score goals by throwing the ball into the opposing team's goal.

Equipment: Two lacrosse goals (either full size or mini—see Things to Make section); cones or shoe polish to mark the crease area, a soft ball that can be thrown with one hand and has little impact, and gym scooters.

Directions:

1. Set up the field of play as shown below. Mark the crease area with shoe polish, floor tape, or cones.

2. Divide the class into teams of about 5-8. Two teams play, each team selecting different colored scooters. The other two teams participate in another activity or in a second game if using half of the gym.

3. Explain the **rules:**
   a. Players may not travel when in possession of the ball.
   b. Players may shoot at the goal at any time.
   c. Players cannot score from inside the crease area.

d. If a player is in possession of the ball and falls off the scooter, he or she quickly gives the ball to the nearest player on the other team for a free throw.

e. Goalies may *not* score. The goalie stands and does not use a scooter.

f. After a score, the goalie of the scored-upon team re-starts play with a free throw.

Variations:

❐ If using a mini-lacrosse goal, using a goalie is not necessary.

❐ If you don't have lacrosse goals, one folding tumbling mat stood on its side works as a goal.

3.22 STAR WARS

Grade Level: 1-8

Description: A throwing/guarding game that is surprisingly active and appeals to the imagination.

Equipment: 4 folding mats or 2 lacrosse goals (with netting); lots of sock balls or lightweight super Nerf™ balls; 2 shields (trash can lids or other devised shields); 2 boards long enough to cover the opening of the goals or mats—2×4 boards will work (place wider side up).

Directions:

1. Place at one end of the gym two folding mats stood on end, locked together to make a semicircular "fort." Place a board in front of the "fort" to keep balls from bouncing out. Repeat at other end of the gym. These are the "Starship Space Stations."

2. Scatter sock and Nerf™ balls in the area. About 40-50 balls are needed.

3. Explain the **rules:**
   a. Two galaxies are at war and are firing "death stars" (sock balls) at each other's Space Stations (the mat forts). Neither army can cross the battle line (the center line of the gym).
   b. Each army has a special guard who stands in front of the Space Station and possesses a "star shield" (the trash can lid) which repels death stars. All warriors may block incoming Death Stars with their bodies.
   c. Warriors may only possess one Death Star at one time and may throw from anywhere on their side of the battlefield.
   d. Death Stars may not be removed from the Space Station until the end of the battle, after they have been counted.
   e. Realism is enhanced by playing the *Star Wars* theme music. When the music stops or when the whistle is blown, both armies must cease fire. Each star shield guard counts all the Death Stars in his or her Space Station. The team that has more Death Stars in its Space Station loses the war.
   f. Change star shield holders and start a new battle.

Suggestions:

❒ Use a small plastic trash can lid with a handle on the back for the "star shield."

❒ Enlarge the separation of the two Space Stations to challenge the throwing ability of the class.

❒ Review good throwing skills, especially the use of opposition when throwing.

3.23 TEAM HANDBALL

Grade Level: 3-8

Description: A very active throwing and catching game played in the gym or on a small hard-court area (about 25′ × 50′); modified from the Olympic game. A definite favorite of mine and the kids.

Objective: To score points by throwing the ball into the opponent's goal.

Equipment: 1 throw-and-catch ball about 6"-7" in diameter that's bouncy, but has little impact; 2 goals, either large lacrosse goals (see "Things to Make" Section 7), or use 2 folded tumbling mats stood upright on their side to make the two goals (see the illustration); scrimmage vests for one or both teams; depending on the type of ball used, you may want protective gear for the goalies

Directions:

1. Mark a crease area around each goal—15 feet out from the sides of the goal for grades 3-5. Increase the distance of the crease from the goal for older students (grades 6-8) to 18-20 feet.

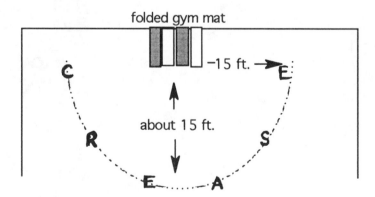

2. Provide scrimmage vests for at least one team (five to seven players per team).

3. Follow regular "Keepaway" **rules:**

a. If tagged while in possession of the ball, the player has three seconds to pass away the ball.

b. Players cannot score after being tagged.

c. Players cannot score from inside the crease area unless they are airborne; that is, they have jumped from outside the crease.

d. After a score, the goalie of the scored-upon team resumes play with a free throw from inside the crease.

e. Defensive players (goalie excepted) should not be inside the crease area. Actually, shots are best stopped from outside the crease.

Suggestions:

❒ Caution students to pick up any ball near a wall by turning their bodies sideways so as to avoid the possibility of accidentally being bumped head first into a wall.

❒ Encourage passes to "open" players.

❒ Encourage deceptive passes and shots. Bounce passes are often the most effective.

3.24 Trashball

Grade Level: 3-8

Description: A fast-paced field game with similarities to lacrosse and basketball.

Objective: To score points by throwing the ball into the opponent's barrel (three points) or by hitting the barrel with the ball (one point).

Equipment: 2 trash barrels (about 30 inches high); team jerseys; a good "throw and catch" ball (a 6"-7" red playground ball works well); cones (or some other way to mark the crease and center line); this game can be played on a grass field or on a hard-court area

Directions:

1. Set up barrels and the field as shown. No side boundaries are needed.

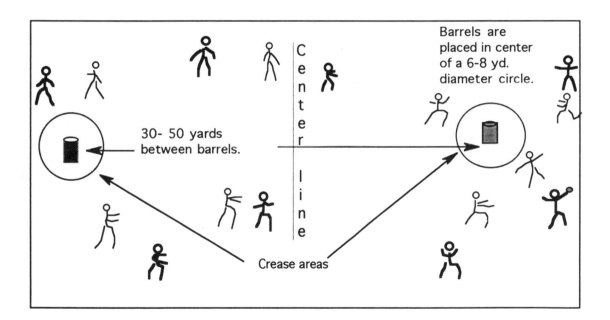

30- 50 yards between barrels.

Barrels are placed in center of a 6-8 yd. diameter circle.

Center line

Crease areas

2. Divide class into *even numbered* teams (eight or ten per team works best.)

3. Give one or both teams colored scrimmage vests.

4. Each team is then subdivided into half on offense, half on defense. Both offense and defense must stay on their half of the center line. The job of the *defense* is to stop the opposing team from scoring and to get the ball over the center line to their offense. The *offense* tries to score from anywhere outside the circle.

5. Explain the **rules:**
   a. As in other "Keepaway" games, the ball carrier must get rid of the ball within three seconds if tagged by an opponent.
   b. A player may not score a goal after being tagged, but may pass to a teammate.
   c. A player cannot score from inside the crease area.
   d. A defense player cannot block a shot from *inside* the crease area; if this occurs, a goal is scored automatically.
   e. Any player may go *through* the crease to get a loose ball.

6. **Scoring:** *One point* is scored for hitting the opposing team's trash barrel with the ball. *Three points* are scored if the ball is thrown into the barrel. After a score, the defense starts play with a free throw from inside their own crease.

Suggestion:

❐ Periodically switch offense and defense players.

3.25 ASTEROIDS

Grade Level: K-8

Description: A fast-action indoor dodge game to use when the lesson includes sock balls or Nerf™ balls.

Objective: To eliminate other players by hitting them with a ball.

Equipment: Lots of Nerf™ balls (the tennis ball sized super-high bounce Nerf™ ball works great in this game)

Directions:

1. Distribute one ball to each player, but extra balls may be scattered on the floor.

2. Explain the **rules:**

   a. The game is started with all players tossing their ball into the air on a signal.

   b. Each player then retrieves a ball (other than his or her own) and begins throwing at other players.

   c. Each player gets three lives. On the first hit, the player goes down to one knee (at the spot where he or she is hit) and can play from that position. On the second hit, the player sits cross-legged on the floor. The third time the player is hit, he or she sits against a side wall and plays from that position.

   d. Players may not travel when kneeling or sitting.

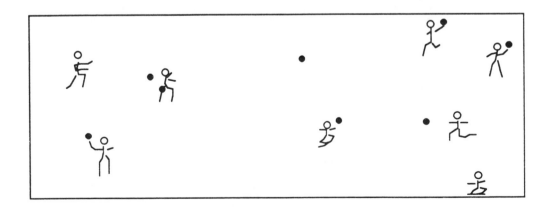

Suggestions:

- ❐ Rather than play until one player remains, start a new game when action slows.

- ❐ This is a wild-looking dodge game, impossible to officiate, so don't even try!

Variation:

- ❐ Any player **catching** a ball out of the air gets to **add** a life. Thus, a player who was sitting, gets to assume a kneeling position, and so on.

3.26 CRACKABOUT

Grade Level: 3-8

Description: A traditional, fast-moving dodge game that uses just one ball and is played in the gym by the whole class. Easy to teach, fun to play.

Objective: To eliminate other players by striking them with a thrown ball and to avoid getting hit by the ball in order to remain in the game.

Equipment: 1 dodge ball (choose a ball that rebounds well off the walls, but can be thrown with one hand and doesn't hurt players who are hit)

Directions:

1. Explain the **rules:**
   a. Players cannot travel when in possession of the ball. If they want to move closer to another player, they may throw the ball so that it bounces off the wall in the direction they wish to go and run to retrieve the ball. Of course, any ball thrown against a wall can be intercepted by another player.
   b. No catching of a thrown ball unless it has first touched a wall or the floor. Players violating this rule are out.
   c. Have the first five players sit out in order of elimination. When additional players get hit out, the players who were eliminated come back into the game in the order they were hit out. In this way no one is out of the game for very long.

2. Throw the ball high against a wall to start the game.

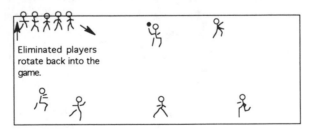

Eliminated players rotate back into the game.

Suggestions:

❏ You may need to demonstrate effective ways to use the walls to travel.

❏ See "Partner Dodge" for a variation of "Crackabout."

3.27 CROSS-OVER DODGE

Grade Level: 1-8

Description: A dodge game in which no one loses. Play this game indoors.

Objective: To win by getting all other players into your court.

Equipment: 3-5 soft dodge balls

Directions:

1. Divide the class into four groups. Groups do not have to be even—divide by birth months or any other criteria that gets approximately even groups.

2. Send each group to one quarter of the gym as shown.

3. Explain the **rules:**

   a. The goal of the game is to get all other players into your section. This is accomplished in two ways: If a player is hit by an air ball, he or she crosses over into the section from which the throw came. If a ball is caught in the air, the player who threw it must cross over into the section of the person who threw the ball.

   b. Players may throw into any of the opposing teams' sections.

Suggestions:

❐ If a section becomes empty, any player may go into that section to retrieve a ball, but must go back into his or her own section to throw.

❐ This game can go on as long as you like. It rarely ends with an outright winner, so it's best used as a warm-up dodge game.

❐ Encourage deception—looking at one team, throwing at another.

3.28 GRASS DODGE

Grade Level: 1-4

Description: If your kids love to play dodge, here's a game for the whole class to play outside on the field. And in this game even those players who are out stay active.

Objective: To eliminate other players by hitting with the dodge ball and to avoid being hit out.

Equipment: 3-4 Nerf™ type balls, light plastic balls or sock balls (you want a ball that is easy to throw, doesn't hurt, and will not travel too far)

Directions:

1. Set up the grass field as shown. Use cones to mark circle. Measure about 15-20 yards across the circle.

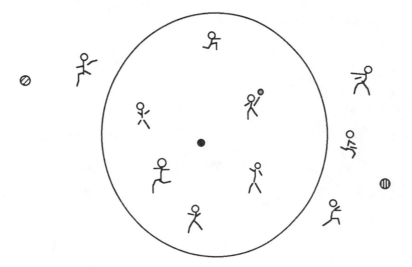

2. Explain the **rules:**
   a. If hit by a dodge ball, a player is out and goes *outside* the circle.
   b. *Inside* players cannot go *outside* to get a ball.
   c. Eliminated players wait *outside* the circle and attempt to retrieve any ball that escapes the circle. If successful in retrieving a ball, the player comes back *inside* as an active player. *Outside* players are constantly trying to hustle and pick up loose balls.

Suggestion:

❐ If too many players are outside the circle, call "New game." The players holding the balls will throw them high into the air on the signal "Go" but may not catch their own ball first. This starts a new game.

Variation:

❐ For older children, do not allow running with the ball.

3.29 PARTNER DODGE

Grade Level: 3-8

Description: "Partner Dodge" is a variation of the standard indoor dodge game (known as "Crackabout"). Both games are very active. In this game each player has a partner of the opposite sex. If the group is uneven, you might end up with two players of the same sex or three players in the last group. In this game when a player is eliminated, the partner is also eliminated from the game!

The last four teams left in the game score points: five points for the winning team, three points for the second place team, two for the third team left, and one point for the fourth team remaining. At the end of several games (games go fast), teams add up their total points to determine the winning teams.

Objective: To eliminate players by hitting them with a dodge ball, and to avoid getting hit in order to remain in the game.

Equipment: 2-3 lightweight dodge balls (use a ball that rebounds well off the wall, but doesn't hurt players when hit)

Directions:

1. Ask students to form boy/girl pairs. Have them sit down when ready so those still standing can choose from remaining students.

2. If students have not previously played "Crackabout," explain the general rules. Then explain the **special rule of "Partner Dodge"**—when one partner is out, both are out.

3. Start the game by throwing the balls into the air; the throwers cannot catch their own balls.

Suggestions:

❑ Encourage passing to the partner (a player cannot get his or her own partner out).

❑ Demonstrate effective ways to use wall passes to travel.

Variation:

❑ *"Ladies Only"*—Only the female partner can eliminate someone. Boys may throw the ball to their girl teammates.

3.30 PIN BOMBARDMENT

Grade Level: 3-8 (with modifications for grades 1 and 2)

Description: An indoor dodge game that has many variations—each is active and among the most favorite activities of kids.

Objective: To win the game by eliminating the other team's players or by knocking over their pins.

Equipment: 6 bowling pins (either plastic or wooden) or plastic milk bottles; 6 dodge balls (easy-to-throw non-stinging balls, slightly deflated plastic balls work, must be throwable with one hand)

Directions:

1. Divide the class into two teams. The quickest and fairest way I know to do this is to ask everyone to get a partner of near equal ability, then split up, going to opposite walls.

2. With grades 3 and 4, try playing across the width of the gym; grades 5 and up, play lengthwise.

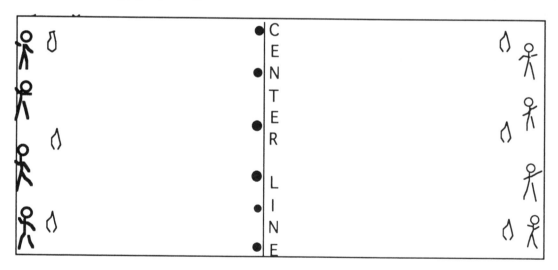

3. Explain the **rules:**

    a. Players are out if they are hit by an air ball, or if a ball they threw is caught in the air by an opposing player.

    b. A ball touching the floor or walls is "safe" to pick up.

c. Players must stay on their side of the center line. Anyone stepping over the center line is also out. Try having the first person eliminated for this reason become the "line judge," watching for other violaters of this rule.

d. Pins may be guarded but not touched. If accidentally knocked down, the pin stays down. If a person guarding the pin is hit, he or she is still eliminated.

e. Eliminated players go to a side wall (or other area) and wait until the end of the game.

f. To start the game, balls are placed on the center line, with players touching the wall behind them (as shown). Alternately, each team could be given an equal number of balls to start.

g. Pins are placed several yards from the walls of the gym (mark the spots on the floor). Adjust pin placement as needed.

Variations:

❒ **Grades 1-3:** *Play across the gym.* For first grade, try placing the pins about 6 yards away from the center line, and about 7 yards away for second grade.

❒ Try these variations after students have played the basic game.
Jailbreak: When eliminated, a player goes *behind* the other team into an area designated as the "jail." Players remain out unless they catch an air ball from a teammate. Kids love to rescue their friends!

Rescue: In this version, anyone catching an air ball gets to bring in one of his or her team's eliminated players back into the game. This greatly encourages catching.

Magic Ball: Use a specially marked ball. If this ball is caught by someone in the jail, *all* their prisoners are freed.

Mystery Dodge: No pins in this variation. Each team secretly selects a mystery player and informs the teacher of their selection. Teams may guard the mystery person, protect a decoy, or use any of a number of stagies. But when this person is hit out, the game is over.

3.31 SHOOTOUT

Grade Level: K-8

Description: This dodge game is reminiscent of an old western shootout. A challenging and exciting way to develop dodging and throwing skills. It can be used as a station or small group activity—good for hot weather.

Objective: To hit an opponent with a ball before you are hit.

Equipment: 4 soft dodge balls (light plastic balls that can be held in one hand are just about right, as are Nerf™ balls or sock balls)

Directions:

1. Players line up as shown:

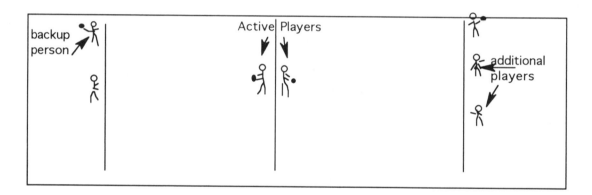

   Two players start in the center of the playing area standing *back to back*. On the signal "Go," they take five quick steps forward (or past a designated line). At this time a player *may* turn and "shoot" (attempt to hit the other player—below the shoulders), or he or she may hold the ball in anticipation of the opponent missing.

2. Players may go anywhere in the playing area and do *not* have to throw at any certain time. After they throw their ball, they may receive a second ball from their backup person (that's the next person in line on their side).

3. Play continues until one player is eliminated. The winner stays to challenge the next player in line. Three wins in a row and the player must "retire as champion" and go to the end of the line.

3.32 SMURF DODGE

Grade Level: K-3

Description: A fitness game for young children that combines running and sit-ups.

Objective: To hit others with a dodge ball transforming them into fat-bellied "Smurfs." When hit, the "Smurf" has to perform five sit-ups to get rid of that fat belly and get back into the dodge game.

Equipment: 2-3 soft dodge balls

Directions:

1. Explain that this is a dodge game in which everyone tries to get a ball and hit others. Any player hit by an air ball turns into an imaginary fat bellied "Smurf."

2. Ask students if they know a good exercise for the stomach muscles. They will likely give the answer, "Sit-ups."

3. To return to the game, the "Smurfs" must first perform five sit-ups.

4. The game is continuous and very active. Participants are either running, throwing, or performing situps.

3.33 SNOWBALL ALLEY

Grade Level: 1-8

Description: An unusual dodge game. Imagine running down an alleyway or road and being bombarded by snowballs from both sides, and you get the idea of this game.

Objective: The throwers attempt to hit the runners with the "snowballs." The runners use evasive tactics to avoid getting hit. This game develops peripheral vision and also the ability to throw at a moving target.

Equipment: Enough sock balls, or other *soft* balls, for half of the class

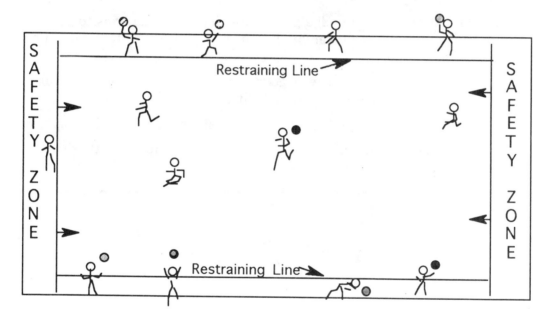

Directions:

1. Divide the class in half. One half goes into one safety zone. The other half splits up, with some players going to each side wall.

2. Distribute a ball to each of the players at the side walls.

3. Explain the **rules:**

    a. Runners try to run from one safety zone to the other safety zone and back again without being hit by a ball. If runners are hit by a ball anywhere between the safety zones, they are out and immediately sit down on the floor.

b. Runners may pause in the safety zone before running back to the original safety zone.

c. The throwers must stay behind the restraining line in front of them. They may throw the ball at any time after the starting signal. They may retrieve any balls that come past their restraining line from the other side.

4. Allow two or three turns for the running team, then have runners and throwers switch places. Balls that are in the center area are returned to the throwing team.

Suggestions:

☐ Remind runners that, when hit, they should sit still on the floor as others may be dodging around them.

☐ Explain how to "lead" a throw in order to hit a moving target.

☐ Play during the winter months as a safe alternative to real snowball fights.

3.34 TUBE DODGE

Grade Level: 1-8

Description: A dodge game that develops strength in the upper body and abdomen.

Objective: To hit others with inner tubes.

Equipment: 3-5 automobile inner tubes

Directions:

1. Tubes must be thrown with an overhead throw and must hit the floor before hitting a player. This makes the hits a little softer.

2. A player cannot throw the same tube twice in a row.

3. Players cannot pick up a tube until it hits someone, hits a wall, or stops rolling.

4. If hit, a player goes to an "out" area. After five players are out, begin sending players back into the game; that is, when the sixth player goes out, the first player out returns.

Suggestions:

❏ Add more inner tubes if action seems slow.

❏ This game may be a little rough for some groups. Caution students ahead of time so that they will not be surprised when hit by a tube.

Variations:

❐ Allow any kind of throw and allow the tubes to hit players in the air. This version can be a little rough, so deflate tubes a bit.

❐ Alternately this game can be played as a *circle game*. Use only two or three tires in this variation. Select two or three players as dodgers to go to the center of the circle. In this variation the player who is hit by a tube switches with the player who hit him or her.

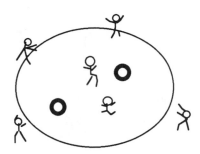

3.35 AEROBIC EASTER EGG HUNT

Grade Level: K-3

Description: Kids won't realize how much running they're doing in this activity until it's over. It makes a good warm-up to some Easter games. It's especially tough if the baskets and the ball area are separated by a hill.

Objective: To collect as many eggs (balls) as possible to add to your team's score.

Equipment: 4 boxes or baskets or colored hoops; 70-100 tennis balls, golf balls, and assorted balls, scattered in a wooded area, somewhat hidden

Directions:

1.   Hide the balls in a wooded or grassy area. Make sure balls are somewhat visible.

2.   Divide the class into four teams. Have each team stand by its box or basket, which is located away from the hidden ball area (20-40 yards is sufficient). Boxes of different colors can become the team's identification. (See the illustration.)

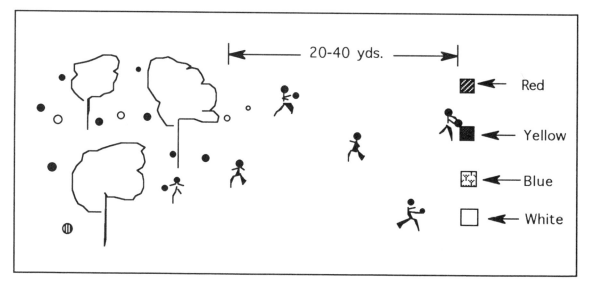

3.   Explain *scoring:* One point for a regular (yellow-green) tennis ball, two points for a colored tennis ball, three points for an odd ball (golf, ping pong, etc.).

4. On starting signal, team members run into the ball area and retrieve *one ball at a time,* and then run back, depositing the balls into their team's basket. Continue until all balls have been found. The team with the highest cumulative score wins.

Suggestions:

❒ At the end of the activity, let the class hide the balls for the next class!

❒ Select one player on each team to count the total points for his or her team.

❒ Adjust the distance to the hidden ball area to fit the needs of the players.

3.36 CHAMPION BALL

Grade Level: 1-6

Description: A very simple basketball game that has been a favorite of students. Even first graders can have success if the baskets are low enough (no more than eight feet high).

Objective: To be the first to shoot a basket.

Equipment: (For each game) 1 basket, 2 balls, 1 floor marker

Directions:

1. Two students face each other opposite the floor marker.

2. The challenger says, "Ready, set, go!" and both players then bounce their ball three times on the floor, quickly touch their basketballs together, and then attempt to be the first to score a basket.

3. The winner (first to score a basket) comes back to the marker as the "champion" and plays the next challenger in line. If a player wins three times in a row, he or she "retires" as champion and must go to another game or to the end of the same line.

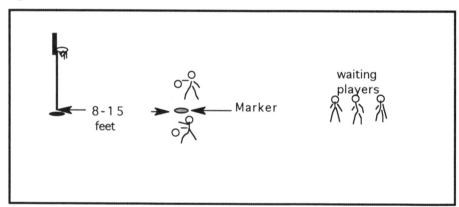

Suggestions:

❐ Use as a shooting game at the end of a basketball class. Play one game at each basket.

❐ Almost every student will win at some time because there is a certain amount of luck involved. But if some players are not winning, set aside one basket for players who have not yet won a game.

3.37 CIRCLE CRAB SOCCER

Grade Level: 1-8

Description: An old favorite activity room game that can be played outside on the grass or in the gym. A good game for postural development and arm strength.

Objective: To kick the cage ball past the opposing team's players.

Equipment: 1 large (36"-48" diameter) cage ball; two traffic cones; jerseys for one or both teams

Directions:

1. Divide the class into two groups, each sitting on opposite halves of the circle as shown.

2. Each team counts off 1-2-3, etc. If there is an extra player on one team, a player on the opposing team gets two numbers. So if Team 1 has eleven players, and Team 2, twelve players, the player on Team 1 is both #11 and #12.

3. Explain the **rules:**

    a. All players must remain in a "crab" position; that is, on hands and feet, facing upward. Players may rest in a sitting position.

b. The teacher/leader will call one (or more) numbers. Players whose numbers are called go inside the circle and attempt to kick the ball past the opposing team's players. All other players remain on the circle as defensive players.

c. Players may not touch the ball with their hands.

Suggestions:

❐ Try to give all players an equal number of turns in the center. It helps to write numbers on a piece of paper and check off the number of turns each player has received.

❐ Caution students about the weight of the ball.

❐ Call in extra players if scoring does not occur in a reasonable time. Each additional player brought into the game also decreases the number of defensive players.

3.38 FLOOR PONG

Grade Level: 3-8

Description: An indoor tennis-type game that enables even third graders to learn and to practice tennis skills successfully.

Objective: To score points, as in tennis, on a modified court.

Equipment: Use almost any kind of paddle: solid plastic paddle rackets, ping pong paddles, racketball rackets, styrofoam "lollipop" paddles, etc. **For each game:** 2 traffic cones (about 18" high); 2 paddles (4 for doubles); 1 bamboo or 1" PVC pole (10-12 feet long); 1 super high-bounce (tennis ball sized) Nerf™ ball

Directions:

1. Prepare courts as shown. The boundaries can be marked in a number of ways, but I like to use shoe polish or floor tape.

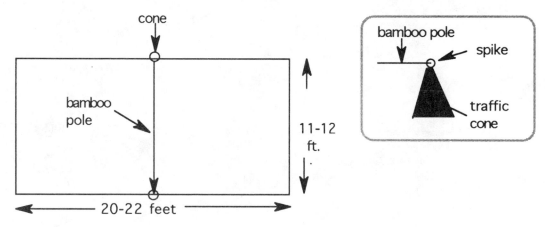

2. Set the bamboo pole on an 18"-high traffic cone. The pole can be further secured by slipping a base-holding spike into the cone and putting the pole through the eye of the base spike (see the diagram).

3. Play *regular tennis rules* with these exceptions:
   a. Underhand drop serve only. Ball is bounced, then served underhanded. This eliminates a smash serve.
   b. *Optional*—After the serve and the return, the ball may be hit out of the air as in regular tennis. Or play *all shots* from a bounce.

c. Play a 7-point game—a point is scored on every serve. A player must win by two points. Players alternate serving after each two points.

Suggestions:

❐ Set up eight to ten courts. Leave a small safety zone (three to four feet) between courts.

❐ Play a tournament (see below) involving the whole class or use just one or two courts as stations.

Variations:

❐ *Tournament play:* Students play a 7-point game. When the game is over, both players go to a designated area. The loser holds up an *"L"* sign with the thumb and index finger and the winner displays a *"W"* sign using the first three fingers. Both will look for players displaying like symbols for their next game.

❐ Have a class tournament ladder (see "Tournament Disks").

3.39 GOODMINTON

Grade Level: K-8

Description: If you find your students are "bad" at badminton, you and your students will love the results when you try "Goodminton."

Objective: To make the skills of badminton easier for young children. Except for the equipment, it's played like the regular game but is easier and much safer.

Equipment: This variation requires the new styrofoam "Lollipop" paddles available through several of the physical education equipment catalogs. These are round paddles with handles of various lengths. I like the 8"-diameter paddle with a 5"-long handle. Use a regular badminton bird with this type of paddle and even small children can successfully practice striking skills.

Directions:

1. Set up the net at about four to five feet high. The net can be a pole set on high jump standards or regular badminton nets. Half of a regular badminton net suspended between two volleyball standards makes a good net.

2. Mark the floor with cones, magic marker, shoe polish, or floor tape. The court dimensions are shown in the illustration.

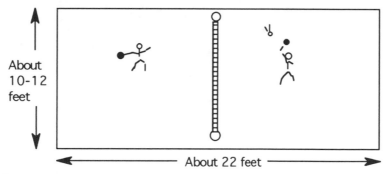

3. Explain regular badminton rules to students. (Remember, this means an underhand serve.)

Suggestion:

❏ With older students, play regulation rules and use this game in tournament play. See "Ladder Disks". Or try a doubles tournament.

3.40 JAKE THE SNAKE

Grade Level: K-6

Description: An old jumping game with a few new twists.

Objective: To stay in the game by jumping over the "snake" as it swings around the circle.

Equipment: A sock; some sand or beans; and a rope or cord

Directions:

1. Fill the toe of a sock with beans or sand. Tie a knot to keep the material in the toe. For a more durable snake, use two socks (one inside the other).

2. Tie a long cord to the end of the sock and draw a snake-like face on the sock.

3. Students stand in a circle around a turner who swings the "snake" around the perimeter of the circle. Students attempt to jump the "snake" as it swings by.

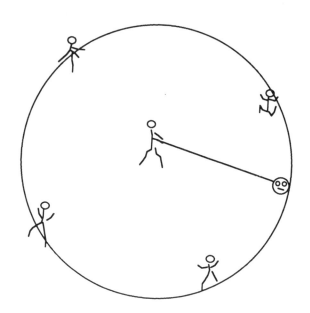

Suggestions:

❑ Remind turners that "snakes don't fly." This keeps "Jake" down on the floor.

❑ *Advice for turners:* Hold the end of the rope in one hand and the other hand down close to "Jake." Then begin by turning your body in a circle while letting out the rope a little at a time.

❑ Play two to three games in a class of 25. Assign a consequence (five push-ups, run around the room, etc.) to be done before returning to a game.

Variations:

❑ Have jumpers **jog** around the circle in the opposite direction of the swinging rope and jump over the snake as they jog.

❑ Take a plastic hockey stick shaft or other plastic tube and stick a jump rope through the tubing. Knot this so the rope will not pull through. Then put some pipe insulation around the tubing (tape it on) and you have a useable "snake" that's easy to turn. We call this our "Pole-ish Snake."

3.41 MULTI-BALL SOCCER

Grade Level: 1-8

Description: Soccer can be a great aerobic game. But for some children it becomes inactive when the ball is often on the other side of the field or the better players get to the ball first. This problem is solved by adding more balls to the game. This, then, is a whole-class activity that increases the activity time, the fitness level, and the soccer skills of all players.

Objective: Same as regular soccer, but additionally to have a great workout (students will self pace), increased skill use, and, of course, increased fun.

Equipment: 1 regular soccer field; scrimmage vests for one or both teams; 2 or more balls (use the softest ball that will work in your game—either slightly deflated regular soccer balls or Nerf™ soccer balls)

Directions:

1. Divide the class into two teams. Then, if you choose, subdivide into an offense and defense or even regular soccer positions.

2. Provide scrimmage vests for one or both teams.

3. Designate (or let students choose) two goalies per team.

4. Explain the **rules:**

3.42 NEVER-OUT

Grade Level: 1-8

Description: This great game comes from the creative brain of my long-time friend Zach Karantonis. It can be played on hard-court, grass, or even indoors. It combines all the skills of diamond games with aerobic conditioning. It will be explained here as a kickball game, but it has many variations.

Objective: To score as many runs in an inning as possible. The fielders try to limit the number of runs by "freezing" the runners.

Equipment: Bases; a marker (for the freeze base); a kickball

Directions:

1. Divide the class into two teams. One team fields, the other bats.

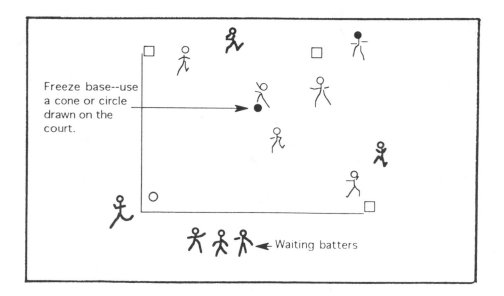

Freeze base--use a cone or circle drawn on the court.

Waiting batters

2. Explain the **rules:**

   a. Each batter (kicker) gets a turn to kick the ball and run the bases. The ball is rolled in by the freeze-base person (the freeze base is located approximately where a pitcher's mound would be).

   b. If the batter doesn't like the roll, he or she may elect to stop, then kick the ball, or ask for another roll.

a. No out of bounds, no penalty kicks, etc.—play is continuous. The teacher will deal with any rule infractions while play continues.

b. If a shot goes through the goal, one of the goalies retrieves the ball and puts it back into play.

c. If a shot goes wide of the goal, any player may retrieve and continue play.

Suggestions:

❒ Add extra balls if play is slow or the class is very large.

❒ Try playing "Multi-Ball Soccer" at the end of a regular soccer class.

Variation:

❒ If teams are not even, try this variation: whenever a player scores a goal, he or she switches to the other team.

3.42 NEVER-OUT

Grade Level: 1-8

Description: This great game comes from the creative brain of my long-time friend Zach Karantonis. It can be played on hard-court, grass, or even indoors. It combines all the skills of diamond games with aerobic conditioning. It will be explained here as a kickball game, but it has many variations.

Objective: To score as many runs in an inning as possible. The fielders try to limit the number of runs by "freezing" the runners.

Equipment: Bases; a marker (for the freeze base); a kickball

Directions:

1. Divide the class into two teams. One team fields, the other bats.

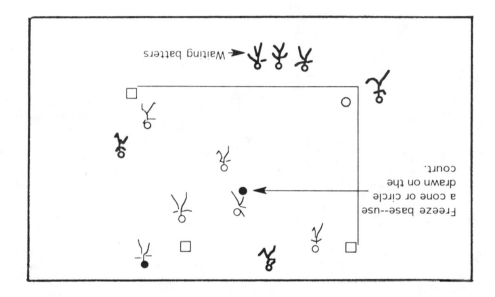

2. Explain the rules:

   a. Each batter (kicker) gets a turn to kick the ball and run the bases. The ball is rolled in by the freeze-base person (the freeze base is located approximately where a pitcher's mound would be).

   b. If the batter doesn't like the roll, he or she may elect to stop, then kick the ball, or ask for another roll.

a. No out of bounds, no penalty kicks, etc.—play is continuous. The teacher will deal with any rule infractions while play continues.
b. If a shot goes through the goal, one of the goalies retrieves the ball and puts it back into play.
c. If a shot goes wide of the goal, any player may retrieve and continue play.

Suggestions:

□ Add extra balls if play is slow or the class is very large.

□ Try playing "Multi-Ball Soccer" at the end of a regular soccer class.

Variation:

□ If teams are not even, try this variation: whenever a player scores a goal, he or she switches to the other team.

c. The batter continues running the bases until the fielders relay the ball to the freeze base, stopping when the freeze-base person yells "Freeze!"

d. When the second batter kicks the ball, **both runners** run the bases, again stopping when the freeze-base person gets the ball and yells "Freeze!"

e. Runners may freeze anywhere on the base path, but not too near home plate. Runners close to home plate should position themselves a few steps away from home plate.

f. This continues until all batters have had a turn to kick—so runners stay on the base paths from the time they kick until the end of the inning. They may cross home plate many times in their running.

3. After all players on one team have batted, the fielding team switches with the batting team.

4. **Additional rules:**
   a. Fielders cannot run with the ball; they must relay the ball to the freeze base. One or two steps are allowed as part of throwing.

   b. The freeze-base person must stay at the freeze base.

   c. Base runners may pass their teammates on the base paths.

   d. Any runner not stopping within a reasonable time must go back to the nearest base.

   e. No one is ever "out," even if the ball is caught in the air.

5. *Scoring:* Each time a runner crosses home plate, he or she scores a run for his or her team. Scores will be high!

Suggestions/Variations:

❑ This game can also be played using: a batting "T"; a pitcher; a Frisbee™; a Nerf™ football; and, for older students, lacrosse equipment.

❑ *Optional:* Place a bowling pin inside a circle. Fielders have to knock over the pin (throwing from outside the circle. to freeze the runners. Best for indoors or hard-surface courts.

❑ Consider rotating three teams—one team fields, one team bats, and one team engages in another activity at the side of the field.

❑ Flip-flop batting order each inning, so that the batter going *first* in the first inning, goes *last* in the second inning.

❑ Have batters line up girl/boy/girl/boy, etc. . . .

3.43 SIX-GOAL SOCCER

Grade Level: 1-8

Description: An outside lead-up game for the whole class. Lots of soccer action and goal tending.

Objective: To score goals against the opposing team and to prevent them from scoring against you.

Equipment: 3 Nerf™ soccer balls; 14 cones; jerseys for at least one team

Directions:

1. Set up field as below—across half of a regular soccer field. Goals are set at about 5-6 paces (yards) between cones.

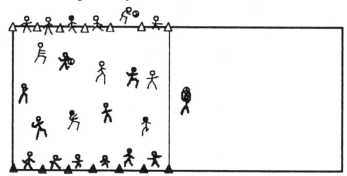

2. Both teams defend their goals and try to score through the other team's goals. Since cones are used to mark goals, goal height is at "goalie's reach." Any ball kicked higher than the goalie can reach is not a goal.

3. Any ball going over a sideline is put back into play with a throw-in by the opposing team.

4. After a period of time, goalies and center players switch places.

Suggestions:

❏ If the class is small, eliminate one or more goals.

❏ If the class is larger, select six goalies (with all others playing as center players); then periodically switch goalies with center players. Play is continuous with goalies returning balls to the field if a score is made.

❏ No score need be kept—just lots of action!

3.44 SWATBALL

Grade Level: 3-8

Description: An aerobic striking game with similarities to volleyball, basketball, and handball. It's played in the gym (or on a small hard-court) with the whole class involved at all times. A definite favorite!

Objective: To hit the ball against the opposing team's wall. The ball must hit below the goalie's highest reach and be inside the designated goal area (usually the entire side wall).

Equipment: Jerseys for one or both teams; one 8"-10" plastic volleyball that's bouncy

Directions:

1. Divide the class into two teams (up to 20 per team in a gym that is about 65' × 50'). Have each team stand against opposite *side* walls.

2. Supply one or both teams with colored jerseys.

3. Each team then counts off 1-2, 1-2, etc., until they have subdivided into an offense and a defense, as shown.

4. Ask both teams' #2 players to step forward. They will be on offense for the first point.

5. The #1's must stay back near the wall. They are the defense. They may move laterally along the wall. Their job is to guard the wall. Any ball touching the wall *below* their highest reach is a score. Any ball hitting *above* the goalie's reach is still in play.

6. The #2's are the offense. They may go anywhere on the floor to try to score against the opposing defense.

7. *All* players may:
   a. dribble the ball as in basketball.
   b. air dribble or "tap up" a ball.
   c. strike the ball with an open hand (as in handball).

   Players may *not:*
   a. kick the ball.
   b. catch the ball.
   c. throw the ball.
   d. fist the ball.

   These rules apply to all players, whether offense or defense.

8. When a goal is scored, offense and defense players change positions and the referee tosses the ball high in the air to start the next point. When any rules infraction occurs, the referee awards a free hit to the opposing team from the point of infraction. Play is continuous.

Suggestions:

❏ If a ball is rolling on the floor, a "scoop up" is allowed. The player may scoop the ball into the air but may not hold the ball.

❏ Sometimes, hitting the ball *down* is the best way to get it *up.*

❏ Using a bouncy, lightweight ball is essential to the success of this game.

Variation:

❏ If the class is small (under 20), you might want to shorten the goal (wall) by taping a jump rope or piece of string on the wall so that it designates the shortened goal.

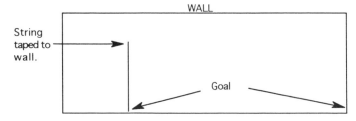

3.45 TRIATHLON

Grade Level: 3-8

Description: An introduction to multi-sport endurance events. Modified for young children with several different variations.

Objective: To be the first to finish the course while performing the three different events. Possible choices are: bicycling, soccer kicking, lacrosse throw and scoop, basketball dribbling, Frisbee™ throwing, and, of course, running.

Equipment: 1 piece of equipment for each contestant in the three events

Directions:

1. To stage an event, set up a circular course (or possibly several courses for the different events). Set up the course something like the illustration.

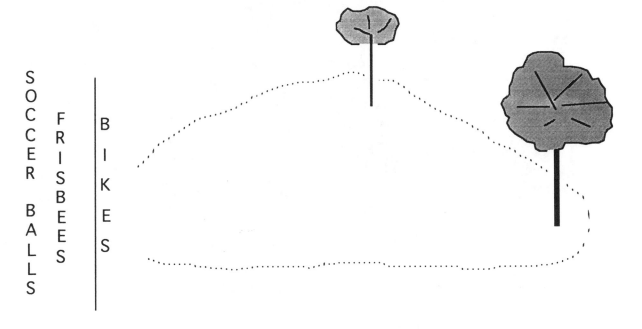

2. Run six to ten triathletes at once. On signal, each participant runs to his or her bike and rides around the tree and back across the line, parking the bike "safely" behind the line.

3. Each player then grabs a Frisbee™, throws the Frisbee™, runs to pick it up, and throws again (no running **with** the Frisbee™!) until back across the line.

4. Then each player gets a soccer ball, kicking it around the tree for a third time. First to finish is the winner. A fun—but tiring—event!

Variations:

❐ After a few tries, have kids group themselves in three's. Students will need to decide who bikes, who throws the Frisbee™, and who kicks the ball. After their portion of the event, they tag their next team member.

❐ Can't work out a triathlon? Try a biathlon!

STRENGTH ACTIVITIES

Your goal should be to include (as often as possible) some sort of strength challenge in every class. As the old saying goes, "Use it or lose it." This is true for kids' muscles as well as for adult muscles. Young children will not get significant gains in muscle size until their teen years, but they can develop strength at any age. And maybe just as important, they will learn how to exert force and learn the techniques of strength exercises.

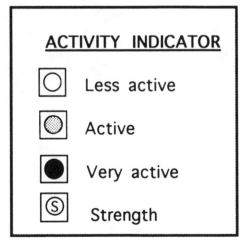

A Word About "Combat Games" (activities 4.10 through 4.18)

Kids love these one-on-one contests; they will even practice them at home with their friends. Some of these have been around for hundreds of years. There is no need to avoid these activities because of the term "combat" or the worry that they will teach aggression. Yes, they do develop a little assertiveness, some of which is necessary for success in life. But consider the other benefits to be gained. Additionally, they develop strength and leverage, and provide a lot of fun.

Suggestions:

❐ One method of having kids play different opponents is to have the winner of each contest hold up the winner's sign (a "W" made by holding up the middle three fingers of one hand). The loser of the match holds up an "L" using the pointer finger and thumb. Both players look for another player exhibiting the same sign to challenge. In this way, eventually all players are likely to win at some time.

❐ Contests are described using the right hand, but lefties should be given the chance to use their preferred hand in some events.

❐ Teach these as a whole class lesson. Then use the activities as a follow-up in a station set-up, including these combat games as well as adding other combat stations such as, "Four-Way Tug," "Kick 'n Hit," or other activities that fit this theme.

❐ Giving clear instructions and insisting on safety procedures will help make combat activities safe and enjoyable.

4.1 TEACHING FITNESS CONCEPTS TO YOUNG CHILDREN

Grade Level: K-3

Description: The concepts of strength and other fitness components can be taught to children as young as 4 and 5 years of age. By using stories and analogies such as those below these concepts will be made clear without a lot of technicalities.

❏ *Milo and the Calf:* Milo lived a long time ago in Greece on a farm. One day, Milo picked up a newborn calf. The animal liked this, so each day Milo would go out and lift the calf. Years went by and quess what happened to Milo? As the calf grew to become a cow, Milo became stronger. In fact, he became the strongest man in his town! As the weight became heavier, Milo gained strength. And this is how all of us gain strength—by working a muscle hard and then resting.

Work + Rest = Strength

Students really enjoy following up this story with attempting to lift a friend. If you have a small hill nearby, the partner can be carried "piggy back" style up the hill. Although a flat area also works, uphill is a tougher challenge and actually safer in the event of a fall. Students are shown how to carry a partner safely on their backs and how to let the partner off at the *top* of the hill. Do not allow carrying down the hill.

❏ *The Valsalva Experiment:* This demonstrates to students the proper breathing for strength. Air should be expelled from the lungs as muscles are exerted. You might use an experiment to teach this principle.

Have all students do a standing long jump and remember their score or mark their spot. Then after a discussion of the Valsalva Effect, ask them to jump again, but this time ask them to *grunt as they jump.* If students are embarrassed to grunt, breathing out hard works the same, but most will love to grunt as they jump. Students will generally jump three to five inches farther. The Valsalva Effect works by tightening the abdominal muscles, thereby transferring power between the upper and lower body—in this case, the arms and the legs. Ask students if they know of any sports in which athletes grunt. They will likely answer weight lifting, karate, tennis, etc. Now they will know why!

❏ *Tennis Ball Squeeze:* When working with tennis balls, ask students to squeeze the ball in one hand until their arm gets tired. (This won't take very long.) Explain that the tennis ball is approximately the size of our heart and that the heart is also a muscle that squeezes, (like our arm muscle does), but it pumps blood that goes to all parts of the body. Explain that the heart must be strong because it never sleeps, never goes on vacation, or stops to really rest. And it does this nonstop for our whole life! Kids are impressed by these facts.

Through questioning of students, bring out the concepts that the heart is strengthened only by aerobic exercise (the expression "huff and puff" helps explain the term "aerobic" to young children). Ask students to name exercises or sports that make us "huff and puff" for long periods of time (5 minutes or longer).

Explain that the heart can likewise be weakened by lack of exercise, a high fat diet, and drugs (including tobacco). And even 5- to 6-year-olds may be damaging their heart muscles if they are not taking care of their hearts.

❐ *Car Analogy:* This teaches the importance of *burning* fuel, not storing it. Explain that our bodies, like cars, use fuel. If we put more fuel (gas) in the car every day, but don't run the car, what happens? The car's fuel tank overflows. Likewise, if we eat more fuel (food), but don't run the engine (body) to burn that fuel, we overflow. And *our* overflow is called *fat*. This brings out the fact that the more active we are, the less likely we are to become fat.

Suggestion:

❐ Often, at the conclusion of some vigorous activities, a cool-down activity is needed. This is a great time to discuss the activity, the fitness benefits of the activity, and bring out fitness concepts with analogies or stories like those above.

Fitness Signs:

❐ It's a great idea to post fitness signs on your gym walls to teach or reinforce fitness concepts. See the following pages for some examples of such signs.

MUSCLES CARRY YOU,
YOU CARRY FAT

TO LOSE FAT
MOVE YOUR FEET !
THE MORE YOU MOVE
THE MORE YOU CAN LOSE

AEROBICS:
EXERCISE   LONGER
NOT HARDER

WANTED:
FITNESS
NOT
FATNESS

FATNESS
IS THE PAST TENSE
OF FITNESS

ENERGY
USE IT OR WEAR IT !

WORK + REST = STRENGTH

FITNESS
USE IT
OR
LOSE IT

Section Four / STRENGTH ACTIVITIES

4.2 PUSH-UP CHALLENGES

Grade Level: K-8

Description: A variety of push-ups to challenge any student. This allows students to select the exercises they prefer or need (as adults do in their fitness programs) and also keeps variety in the class. Always a great upper-body exercise.

Objective: To add variety to a very beneficial exercise so that students will find the exercise more interesting and challenging.

Variations:

- ❐ Modified push-up—The performer does the push-up from the knees instead of the toes. This variation is mostly for those who cannot perform regular push-ups.

- ❐ Hands placed very wide apart—especially good for the chest muscles.

- ❐ Hands placed very close together—especially good for the triceps.

- ❐ Fingertip push-up—extra benefit to the forearm and hand muscles.

- ❐ Fist push-ups.

- ❐ Handstand bar push-ups—See Section "Things to Make."

- ❐ Marine push-up—From a prone position, push vigorously and clap hands together before catching the body with arms in an extended position.

- ❐ Seal push-up—Same as Marine push-up, but click heels and clap hands.

- ❐ Popsicle push-up—a group effort. This is a little tricky to get into and requires group cooperation, but it's quite an accomplishment if completed. Each person places his or her feet on the back of one person and also has another person's feet on his or her back.

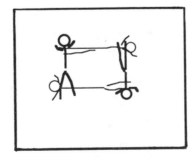

4.3 SIT-UP CHALLENGES

Grade Level: K-8

Description: A variety of exercises to challenge the abdominal fitness of all your students no matter what their fitness level.

Objective: To have all students, regardless of their fitness level, benefit from abdominal exercises.

Variations:

❐ **For students who cannot do regular sit-ups** (knees bent, arms folded, hands on opposite shoulder), try these modified sit-ups:

a. *Pull-up/Sit-up:* Students assume the standard position except they grasp the sides of their shorts or slacks and pull as they sit up.

b. *Curl-ups or Crunches:* Normal position, but instead of coming all the way up as in regular sit-ups, the performer just curls the body up as far as possible before returning to the floor.

c. *Swing-ups:* Assume normal position, but extend arms overhead on the mat. The performer swings his or her arms, which assists in bringing the body to a sit-up position.

❐ Advanced abdominal challenges:

a. *Jackknife:* The performer lies stretched out on the mat on her or his back and attempts to jackknife (bringing straight arms and straight legs up to meet above the body).

b. *Leg lifts:* Performers lie back with hands placed under the buttocks (to protect the back). Lift feet a few inches off the floor and hold as long as possible.

Suggestions:

❐ Explain to students the importance of abdominal strength. Some of the benefits of good abdominal fitness include:

— Providing a strong protective cover or shield for vital organs, thus protecting the organs from harm in an accident.

— Acquiring better posture.

— Helping to avoid back problems.

— A strong, flat stomach looks better.
— Strong stomach muscles are beneficial in every sport.

❏ Explain to students that the stomach muscles are actually three parts: the upper stomach, developed by regular sit-ups; the lower stomach, developed by leg lifts; and the sides of the stomach, developed by twisting movements.

4.4 CHIN-UP CHALLENGES

$\boxed{\text{S}}$

Grade Level: K-8

Description: A variety of chin-ups to challenge all levels of fitness.

Variations:

❏ *Regular Chin-up:* For average students, the *overhand bar grip* is preferred because it utilizes a greater number of muscles. Chin-ups use many of the muscles from the waist up. The overhand grip is also closer to the grip used more often in sports.

❏ *Bent Arm Hang:* Many students who cannot do chin-ups find they can get the same strength benefits from a bent arm hang (with the chin positioned over the bar).

❏ *Jump Chin:* Place the chinning bar about even with the top of the head of the student, or a bit higher. The student grasps the bar and uses a *jump and pull* to get his or her chin over the bar, lowering slowly back down. Repeat.

❏ *Gravitron Chin:* Many health clubs have a machine that has a platform for an exerciser to stand on. The performer grasps a chin-up bar and, with the help of the machine which raises the platform, does chin-ups. This makes chin-ups possible for anyone. Kids can do the same by having one or more friends assist them in doing a chin-up. Just a light lift on the legs is all most students need. Caution helpers to *stop helping quickly* when the performer chooses to stop. The teacher might choose to spot this activity for a while.

4.5 CREATIVE EXERCISE CHALLENGES

Grade Level: K-8

Description: A variety of fun-to-do strength exercises that especially appeal to young children.

Variations:

❐ *Blast Off (K-5):* An activity that teaches the standing long jump and develops leg strength in an enjoyable way.

 a. Have all students stand with toes on a straight line facing in one direction.

 b. Ask students to raise arms overhead.

 c. Begin a countdown backwards from ten to one. Students will progressively lower their arms and flex their knees, achieving the standing long jump take off position by the count of "One."

 d. After the count of "One," call out "Blast off!" and all students will attempt to jump forward as far as possible in a standing long jump.

 e. The illustration shows the position of the arms and the leg flexion relative to the countdown.

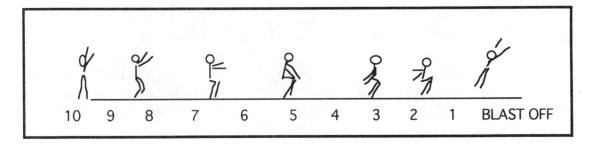

Suggestions for "Blast Off":

❐ Use as a cool-down activity right before dismissal from class.

❐ Try as a lead-up to a future track-and-field unit or a fitness-testing class in which the long jump will be done.

❐ Encourage students to swing their arms vigorously forward as they jump.

❐ See activity 4.1 for use of the Valsalva Effect in jumping.

- ❏ **_Triple Jump:_** Have students stand with one foot on a line. Instruct them to:
  - a. Hop forward onto the same foot (maintain balance).
  - b. Take a long step forward to the other foot (maintain balance).
  - c. Finally jump forward from the foot in step #2, landing on both feet to finish.
  - d. Do slowly a few times, then without pausing between jumps, and finally with a run to the take-off line.

- ❏ **_Butt Busters (1-8):_** The student sits with feet toward a wall. The student places his or her hands on the floor, and the feet up on the wall. Using arm and abdominal muscles, the student lifts his or her bottom off the floor and repeats.

- ❏ **_Dippers (K-8):_** The student lies back and places both hands on a folded mat with fingers facing toward his or her feet, which are extended out in front. The student pushes up from the floor to an extended arm position above the mat, then lowers down and repeats.

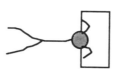

- ❏ **_Jump-Ups (K-8):_** The student stands on the floor with his or her feet near a folded mat that is placed against a wall. The student begins jumping up onto the mat and back down, landing on two feet and keeping his or her hands on the wall for support.

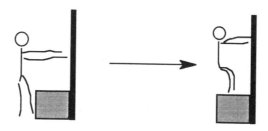

4.6 POLE VAULT

(S)

Grade Level: K-8

Description: A strength-building activity that kids will do over and over because it's so much fun. And it really does mimic the actual event of pole vaulting.

Objective: To use a knotted rope to jump over a high jump cross bar.

Equipment: A piece of thick jump rope or mountain climbing rope (about 10 feet); a sturdy pole for attaching the rope, such as a basketball support, an outside chin-up bar, or even a sturdy horizontal tree branch; high jump standards and a cross bar (An inexpensive and adequate cross bar can be made with two round plastic hockey stick shafts. Fasten shafts together with a piece of wooden dowel wedged into the joined ends. Tape over the joined section.)

Directions:

1. Fold the rope in half and, starting at the open ends of the rope, begin knotting with simple overhand knots every five to seven inches. These knots give the jumper a better grip of the rope. Leave the top two feet unknotted so that you can just throw this top loop over a support and stick the ends of the rope through the loop to secure the rope.

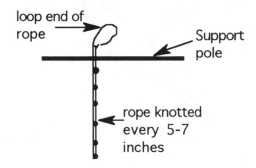

loop end of rope

Support pole

rope knotted every 5-7 inches

2. Place the high jump standards so that the bar is directly beneath the hanging rope. NOTE: If the rope is too long, jumpers can fold the rope as they grasp it.

3. Place a mat or pad on the other side from the jumper just to make landings softer. NOTE: Performers will land on their feet.

4. Explain to jumpers that they can get over the bar any way they choose, using the rope. Some will jump backward and swing to the bar, some

will go over sideways, some backwards. Some swing will be necessary, however. But in all styles, upper body strength is used to lift the body over the bar.

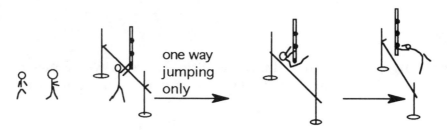

one way
jumping
only

Suggestions:

❏ Use as a station with the bar set at a challenging height.

❏ Have a contest, moving the bar gradually up until one jumper remains.

4.7 ROPE PULL RACES

Grade Level: K-8

Description: During a gymnastic unit, we often have children who are unable to climb the vertical rope. This is generally due to insufficient strength or technique, but some students are unable to climb due to fear of heights. Whatever the reason, these students feel left out and, in fact, are left out, of a very beneficial strength building activity. Here's a solution that is fun, competitive, adds another station to your program, and is still beneficial for students. And there is absolutely no chance of falling in this variation!

Objective: To develop upper body strength.

Equipment: A strong rope, such as a tug-o-war rope or mountain climbing rope, and somewhere sturdy to fasten the rope (the foldout-type gymnastic ladders work well); a folded mat or other cushion to protect students at the end of their pull

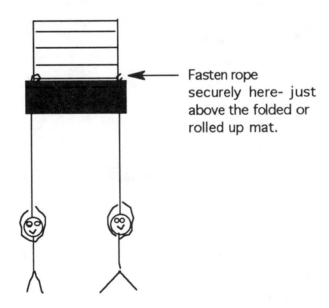

Fasten rope securely here- just above the folded or rolled up mat.

Directions:

1. Loop the rope several time around the bars of the ladder to secure, then stretch rope out on the floor so that both sides of the rope are the same length.

2. Place a folded mat against bars to protect students.

3. Students grasp the rope while lying on their backs. On a signal they pull on the rope, attempting to be the first to pull themselves to the finish at the mat. No use of feet allowed.

Suggestion:

❏ To avoid getting clothing dirty from being dragged on the floor, place two carpet squares on the floor. Students place their bodies on the carpet instead of the floor.

Variations:

❏ *Commando Pull:* Participants lay in a prone position.

❏ *Genie Pull:* Participants maintain a sitting position throughout the race.

4.8 TARZAN SWING

Grade Level: K-8

Description: This activity appeals to just about everyone, but is especially beneficial to those students who lack sufficient strength to climb a rope.

Objective: To swing from one perch to another using a regular climbing rope.

Equipment: A climbing rope that swivels at its attachment (the rope, when it swings, should not put pressure on the sleeve that holds the rope. The whole sleeve and rope should swing from the metal attachment. If the sleeve does not swivel, swinging will put pressure on the rope; this is not recommended.); 2 stacked folded mats or low vaulting boxes on each side for students to stand on; mats under the area of swinging

Directions:

1. Place a folded mat or low vaulting box on each side of the matted area. Test swing to determine how far apart to place the boxes.

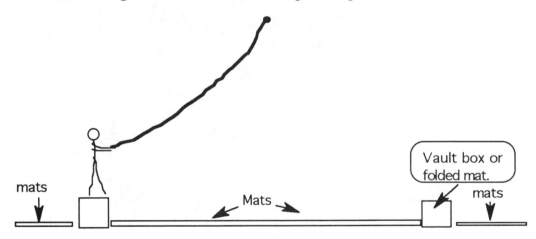

2. A student stands on one box, grasps the rope (holding as high as possible), and swings across the area to the other box.

Suggestions:

❏ For a little imagery, tell students that the area between the boxes is quicksand, an alligator pit, or poisoned peanut butter!

☐ Nearly all students are able to hang onto a rope while swinging, thereby gaining in strength. And it's so much fun, they'll repeat often.

☐ Use as a station, as part of an adventure program, or as a change in your gymnastics program.

Variation:

☐ *Pick Up* (1-8): Place a plastic bowling pin (or similar object) at the far end of the rope swing. **The challenge for students:** Swing over and pick up the pin with their feet and return to the starting point. Great for abdominal strength. Place mats under the swinging area.

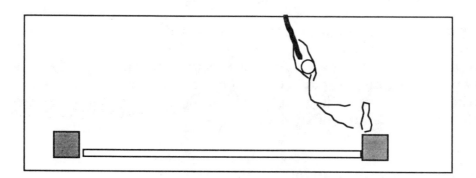

4.9 BATMAN BOWLING

Grade Level: 1-8

Description: A challenge that tests arm and abdominal strength and is so much fun kids will try this over and over.

Objective: To knock down the bowling pins while swinging on the rope.

Equipment: Climbing rope; mats; 6 or 10 plastic bowling pins (or six 2-liter plastic soda bottles)

Directions:

1. Place six or ten bowling pins at the far end of the rope swing area in a bowling pin arrangement. Mark pin locations with magic marker.

2. Place mats between the take-off point and the bowling pins. Place some sort of barrier around the pins so they will be contained when kicked. Folded mats stood on end will work.

3. Explain the *challenge:* Swing over and knock down as many pins as possible.

4. Allow one or two swings depending on how far apart pins are placed. Make sure all pins are within reach of most students. Pins may be kicked into other pins as in regular bowling.

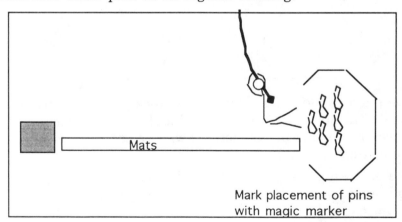

Mats

Mark placement of pins with magic marker

Suggestion:

❏ Mark *two* sets of pin placements on the floor; one for grades 1 and 2, one for older children.

4.10 QUICK HANDS

Grade Level: 1-8

Description: A good way to begin a lesson on combat games, as this activity teaches the meaning of the terms **offense** and **defense.** This activity stresses quickness.

Objective: The attacker attempts to successfully slap the back of the defender's hands. The defender attempts to avoid this slap.

Equipment: Spread out mats to make a large, cushioned, rectangular area

Directions:

1. Players may stand or sit to play this contest.
2. The player on offense places his or her hands out in front with the palms facing up.
3. The player on defense places his or her hands lightly on top of the offense player with palms down.

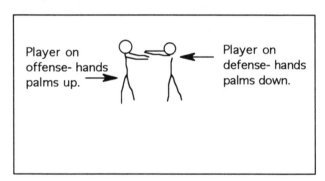

4. The player on offense attempts to quickly (and lightly) slap the top of the defense player's hands and wins if he or she does so. If the defense player moves his or her hands away before the slap, that player wins the contest.
5. The defense player loses if his or her hands are slapped or if he or she pulls hands away before the offense player moves.

Suggestions:

❐ Have the two players switch positions.

❐ Encourage light and quick slaps.

4.11 LEG WRESTLING

Grade Level: 1-8

Description: A test of leg strength and leverage. It's even fun for the person getting flipped over.

Objective: Each player attempts to pull the opponent over with their leg.

Equipment: Mats

Directions:

1. Opponents lay on their backs with the right sides of their bodies against one another—so each is lying in the *opposite* direction on the mat. The key position is for both partners to *interlock elbows.*

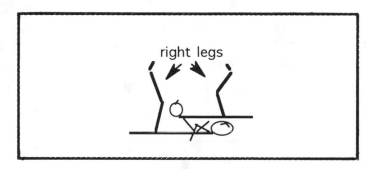

2. Both players lift their inside (right) leg on the count of "One," then lower the leg, raise the leg again on "Two," lower it again. Then, on the count of "Three," each player's leg goes past the opponent's leg, hooking the leg at the knee. Both players then attempt to pull their opponent over by pulling with their leg.

4.12 PUSH-UP PULL

Grade Level: 1-8

Description: A contest in which balance, strength, and quickness are all needed to win.

Objective: To cause the opponent to fall from the push-up position.

Equipment: Mats

Directions:

1. Both players assume a push-up position facing each other on the mat (as shown).

2. On the starting signal, each player attempts to cause the opponent to touch a knee to the mat or fall to the mat (falls do not hurt from this height). They can do this by pulling on the opponent's arm. The opponent can also pull an arm away in defense. Sometimes this defensive move causes the attacker to fall.

3. Players may move around the mat, but must stay in the push-up positions.

4.13 NATIVE AMERICAN HAND WRESTLING

Grade Level: 1-8

Description: A contest that requires strength, but also balance and deception.

Objective: Both players use strength and skill to cause the opponent to move a foot.

Equipment: Mats

Directions:

1. The two players shake hands and maintain the handshake while positioning their feet in a stable stance. The *outside edge* of a player's right foot should be placed against the *outside edge* of the opponent's right foot.

2. On the starting signal, each player attempts to cause the other to move either foot. This is done by pushing, pulling, and faking moves that cause the opponent to lose balance and, therefore, move a foot. Mats are not essential for this activity, but do provide an extra measure of safety. Players should not fall to the floor. The idea is to cause the opponent to lose balance, not to fall to the floor.

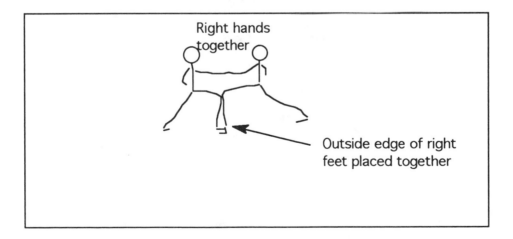

4.14 ARM WRESTLING

Grade Level: K-8

Description: Another traditional combat game. This one even has national championships!

Objective: Each player attempts to force the other's hand to the mat.

Equipment: Mats

Directions:

1. Partners lay prone on the mat, facing each other.
2. They grasp right hands (hooking thumbs, actually) with arms at a 90-degree angle, and their elbows on the mat.
3. Instruct both students to place their other arm behind the elbow that is placed on the mat. This helps keep elbows from sliding on the mat.
4. On the starting signal, each partner attempts to push the opponent's hand to the mat. Players must keep their elbows on the mat.

Right hands locked at the thumbs.

Left hands crossed under the right arms.

4.15 HOLD 'EM BACK

Grade Level: 1-8

Description: A combat game that develops wrestling skills and strength.

Equipment: Mats; designated finish line

Objective: For the player in front to crawl across the designated finish line in a certain time period, while the player in back wins if he or she stops the front player from reaching the goal.

Directions:

1. Both players assume a kneeling position on the edge of the mat, one behind the other as shown.

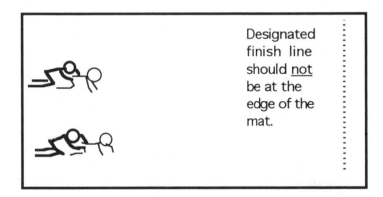

Designated finish line should <u>not</u> be at the edge of the mat.

2. Set a time standard, depending on the length of the mats. For instance, a one-minute time period is given for the front player to reach the designated goal line. If the back player succeeds in keeping the front player from reaching that goal, then the back player wins.

3. On the starting signal, the player who is in front attempts to crawl to a designated finish line across the mats. The player behind tries to hold back the front player by maintaining a grip on legs or waist, not clothing.

4. Switch positions so the back player gets a turn in front.

Suggestion:

❑ Stress keeping the action safe and avoiding unnecessary roughness.

4.16 REACH AROUND

Grade Level: 1-8

Description: A contest of quickness on the mat.

Objective: Each player attempts to maneuver behind the other and grab the opponent's jersey.

Equipment: Strips of cloth or scrimmage jerseys for each player; mats

Directions:

1. Opponents kneel on the mat facing each other. Each has a strip of cloth or a jersey tucked into the back of his or her pants.

2. On the starting signal, both players attempt to be the first to pull out the other's jersey.

3. Players must stay in a hands and knees position, but may move around on the mat.

Suggestion:

☐ Stress keeping the hands on the mat except when grabbing for the flag.

4.17 JOUSTING

Grade Level: K-8

Description: An activity that's fun at any age. It develops strength and strategy, and can be played on grass or in the gym with mats for padding.

Objective: To cause your opponent to fall off the tire.

Equipment: 2 tires (preferably wide, small truck tires); a 5- to 6-yard length of either mountain climbing rope or strong nylon webbing (strong jump rope material will also work, but webbing is the best); mats if inside

Directions:

1. Each participant stands on top of a tire with an equal amount of excess webbing as shown.

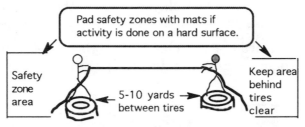

2. To start the contest, either player calls out "Ready," the other player answers "Set," and then the first player says "Go." Each player then attempts to cause the other to fall off the tire by:

   a. Tugging on the rope to pull the opponent off the tire.

   b. Releasing the rope to cause the opponent to fall backwards.

3. **Special situations:**

   a. If Player A completely lets go of the rope, but *does not* cause Player B to fall off, then Player A loses.

   b. If Player A lets go of the rope, but Player B *does* fall off, then Player A wins.

Suggestion:

❐ This game requires strategy as much as strength. Good strategy involves making fake releases and pulls, and not ever completely releasing the rope unless absolutely sure the opponent will fall off the tire.

4.18 GO BEHIND

Grade Level: 3-8

Description: A fast moving combat game requiring strength and quickness.

Objective: For the free player to get behind and grab onto another player. The pair of players attempts to move quickly so that no free player latches onto the back of them.

Equipment: Mats provide extra protection, but aren't necessary because no one should fall in this contest

Directions:

1. Demonstrate this contest. Ask one player to grab another from behind around the waist. Fingers should not be interlaced but cupped and locked together. The back player controls the pair; his or her goal is to keep anyone else from latching onto his or her waist.

2. Pair up two-thirds of the class. The other one-third are free players. They will roam around attempting to grab onto the waist of one of the pairs.

3. If a free player manages to grab onto the back of a pair, he or she takes over at the back of the pair and the front player in the pair becomes a free player.

Suggestion:

❐ If not enough players are successful at grabbing on, break up a few pairs to increase the number of free players.

4.19 PARACHUTE BASKETBALL

Grade Level: K-8

Description: Many parachute activities are great for developing upper body strength and are definitely near the top of the fun list of young students.

Objective: To cause your team's ball to go through the inner tube thus scoring a basket.

Equipment: 1 automobile inner tube or hula hoop; 2 balls of different color, but otherwise alike; parachute

Directions:

1. Divide the class into two groups (this may be boys vs. girls if you like). Groups do not have to be separated; they can be anywhere around the chute.

2. Place a small auto inner tube on top of the parachute (a hula hoop will work—but not as well). Also place two different colored balls on the chute—one for each team.

3. Designate which team will be shooting which ball.

4. On starting signal, each group tries to shake the chute, causing *their* ball to go through the tube. The ball may go through the tube in any direction.

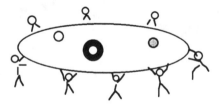

Suggestion:

❏ Keep the game short as arms get tired quickly in this one. The first team to get three baskets might be enough.

4.20 PARACHUTE SLED RIDE

Grade Level: K-2

Description: Kids won't know this is a strength activity unless you tell them because it's so much fun. It's the thrill of a fast sled ride without the danger.

Objective: To pull the parachute quickly across the room to give the riders a "sled ride."

Equipment: 1 parachute in good condition

Directions:

1. Select one to three students to *sit or kneel* on top of the parachute, which is spread out at one end or corner of the gym. The remaining students go to the other side of the parachute and, on signal, pull the parachute (and its riders) to the other end or corner of the gym.

2. Select new riders. The pullers now go to the opposite end of the parachute to start the next pull.

Suggestions:

❏ Caution pullers to avoid falling down as they are pulling. Falling is best avoided by pulling with one hand only and running forward, not backward.

❏ For a longer ride, pull the parachute from corner to corner.

4.21 PARACHUTE TUG-O-WAR

Grade Level: K-3

Description: A simple strength activity for the upper body.

Objective: To pull the parachute towards you as in any Tug-o-War.

Equipment: 1 parachute in good condition (if there are small rips near the handles of your chute, ask students to roll the edges of the chute slightly before pulling)

Directions:

1. Have all students sit with their legs under the stretched-out parachute.

2. With a strong grip, students try to pull the parachute toward them in a rowing motion. This also can be called "Row, Row, Row Your Boat." Everyone does not have to pull in the same direction.

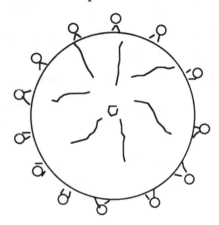

Suggestion:

❐ Use as a quick strength builder between other parachute activities.

4.22 BIG FAN

S

Grade Level: K-8

Description: The perfect activity to use when students begin to overheat. One group gets a break while the others still develop strength.

Objective: To use the parachute as a giant fan and cool off the group that is lying under the parachute.

Equipment: 1 parachute

Directions:

1. Ask students to count off by four's (or other number of your choice) as they stand holding the parachute.

2. Explain that when the parachute is lifted, you will call out a number. All students having that number will go under the parachute and lie flat on their backs.

3. The remaining students will make giant waves with the parachute, creating a breeze for those lying on the floor.

4. Repeat until all numbers have been called.

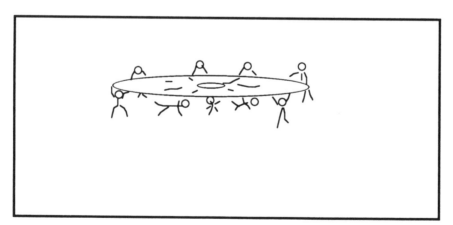

Suggestions:

❐ Do this activity toward the end of a parachute session to give students a short break. Parachute activities do stress the arm muscles quite a bit.

❐ This activity is especially welcome on a hot summer or fall day.

4.23 ROLL UP

Grade Level: K-8

Description: Even putting the parachute away can be made into a strength developer with this activity.

Objective: To roll up the parachute in preparation for putting it away (and getting exercise in the process). This teaches the meaning of the term "Going for the burn."

Equipment: 1 parachute

Directions:

1. Do this activity when it's time to pack the chute away for the day.

2. Ask students to pull the parachute until it's tight.

3. Instruct them to begin rolling the edge of the parachute using an overhand grip. They will be pulled toward the center. Ask them to "roll your way in; make the parachute pull you in." Instruct them not to just walk in. As students are rolling the chute, explain that they will begin to feel a mild burning sensation in their forearms. Explain that this means their muscles are working really hard and will get stronger from this.

4. When the group has rolled their way almost to the center, select several students to collect it and place it in the storage box or bag while the others line up for dismissal.

4.24 FOUR-SQUARE CAGE BALL

Grade Level: 1-8

Description: An enjoyable way to end a tumbling class. After using arm muscles, it's a welcome change to use the legs.

Objective: To kick the ball over the mat of another team.

Equipment: 1 large (36"-42") cage ball; four mats

Directions:

1. Place four mats in a square with the inside edges touching, as shown.

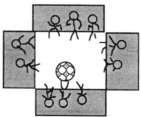

2. Divide the class into four teams. Players sit on the inside edge of each mat, facing inward. They should lie back, resting on their elbows. Explain that each group is to attempt to kick the cage ball over the heads of one of the three other teams.

3. Explain other **rules:**

   a. Each team starts with five points. If the ball goes over a mat, the team on that mat loses one point. The game is over when one team has lost all of its five points. The team(s) with the most points remaining wins.

   b. If the ball goes out at a corner, no team loses points.

Suggestions:

❐ For an exciting way to start each game point, have the team members nearest the ball lie down flat on their mat; the person with the ball rolls the ball over the supine bodies into the center of the square. That team quickly sits up and the game point is begun.

❐ If players leave the edge of the mat and move forward into the center, remind them that (1) the rest of their team doesn't get to help, and (2) the other teams can more easily kick the ball over their heads.

4.25 MAGIC CARPET RIDE

⬡ S

Grade Level: 1-2

Description: A strength builder for young children that's also a great cooperative learning activity.

Objective: To help each of the team members experience the magic carpet ride.

Equipment: 1 mat for each 7-9 students

Directions:

1. Students form groups of seven to nine.
2. Students take turns giving each other a "magic carpet ride" by holding the handles or sides of a **flat** (not folding) **tumbling mat.** The rider sits on the mat as he or she is carried about the room.

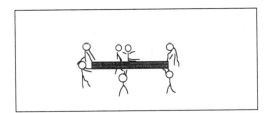

Suggestions:

❐ This is a strenuous activity. Short and equal turns for each group member is the key.

❐ Caution students to let down the rider easily.

4.26 MAT RACES

Grade Level: K-8

Description: These races combine skill, strength, and speed.

Objective: To race across the mat as quickly as possible.

Equipment: 11 or more mats

Directions:

1. Set up mats in rows of at least three mats, end to end, to form "lanes," as shown.

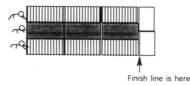

Finish line is here

2. Students form lines behind the rows of mats. Try to have at least three or four lanes of mats.

3. In each race, the first performer to reach the finish line is the winner. Participants must stay in their designated lane of mats.

4. Possible mat race contests:

   a. **Seal Walk**—No use of the legs allowed. Legs are dragged using the arms.

   b. **Crab Walk**—Performers start with feet over the edge of the mats and go head first. Bottoms are allowed to touch the mat. Racers will often stumble in this one, which makes it exciting.

c. **Reverse Crab Walk**—Racers go feet first. This one is tough!

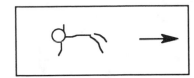

d. **Crawling**—Racers must be on hands and knees. This race moves extremely fast and is a lot of fun.

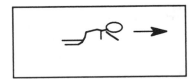

e. **Somersault**—Racers do rolls down the mat. Dive rolls are allowed.

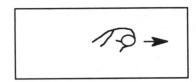

f. **Chariot or Pyramid Races**—Two students kneel on the mat, side by side. A third student kneels on the backs of the first two. To win the race, the top person must stay on top. Any body part of the top person touching the mats causes disqualification.

Suggestions:

❏ Remind students to walk *around* the mats as they return to one of the lines for their next race.

❏ Hold championships, such as a crawling championship. *Example:* You might have several heats (those born in January/February race first, then March/April, and so on). Then have the six winners race for the championship. Mix up these championships in creative ways so each one is different.

4.27 WHEELBARREL

Grade Level: K-8

Description: A traditional exercise (with a few variations) that happens to be excellent for developing strength of the upper body at almost any age.

Objective: For the two partners to execute the wheelbarrel.

Equipment: Mats

Directions:

1. Demonstrate the standard wheelbarrel. One partner lies prone on the mat. His or her partner lifts feet as he or she pushes to extended arms. NOTE: The standing partner simply follows the bottom partner and **does not push.**

2. The partners change positions, reversing roles.

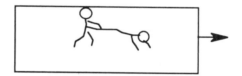

Suggestions:

❐ The wheelbarrel can be done as a warm-up activity for mat races, but **should not be done as a race** because of the possible injury to the bottom person when racing. The standing person should **follow—rather than push**—the bottom person.

❐ Stress staying on the mat. When the bottom person nears the end of the mat, he or she may roll out by tucking the head under or simply step down.

Variations:

❐ **Upside Down Wheelbarrel**—The bottom partner faces upward.

❐ **Handwalk Wheelbarrel**—The standing partner lifts the bottom person's feet and places them on his or her shoulders as the bottom person handwalks.

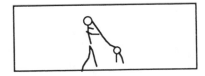

❐ **Two-Way Wheelbarrel**—You will need a very strong person in the center. This person first lifts the feet of a partner facing away from his or her back, then lifts the feet of another who is facing away from his or her front.

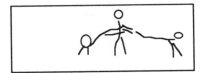

ACTIVE STATIONS

Stations are fun for both teachers and students. They allow teachers the opportunity to offer individual help to students. If a team game is being played that does not involve all students, stations can be used to keep those students not playing involved in a worthwhile activity.

Usually you want students to move to all stations during a class period, but sometimes it's a nice change for students to have the option to select just those activities that interest them most.

Many of the games and other activities in this book can also be used in a station set-up.

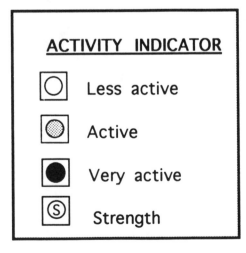

5.1 BASKETBALL GOLF

Grade Level: 3-8

Description: A unique warm-up shooting activity (or competitive basketball game) that will challenge the shooting ability of your students. This is obstacle course basketball shooting.

Objective: As in all golf games, to shoot the holes (in this case, baskets) with the fewest number of shots.

Equipment: As many baskets (regular or created) as you can set up (a basket can be used for two different holes if baskets are limited); 1 basketball for each group; score cards and pencils

Directions:

1. Make up score cards as shown—have one score card and one pencil for each group. (See Section 10, "Ready-to-Use Forms," for a master form.)

Basketball Golf	Name #1	Name #2	Name #3	Name #4
Hole #1				
Hole #2				
Hole #3				
Hole #4				
Hole #5				
-Continue to 9 holes-				

2. Mark starting lines on the floor with tape, permanent magic marker, shoe polish, etc. Draw an arrow pointing to the basket to be shot.

3. Explain general **rules** of the activity:
   a. The ball must be played from where it is caught. As the ball rebounds off an obstacle or basket, students will hurry to catch it, then take their next shot from that location.
   b. Students will record the number of shots needed to make the basket on their group's score card.

4. Divide the class into small groups (two to four per group). The whole class plays at once, but all groups do not have to start at the #1 basket. Some would start at #2, some at #3, etc.

5. Describe the course, showing starting points, type of shot, etc.

6. Direct students to get one score card and one pencil per group and begin.

7. Here is an example of a basketball golf course set up in a gym. Be creative!

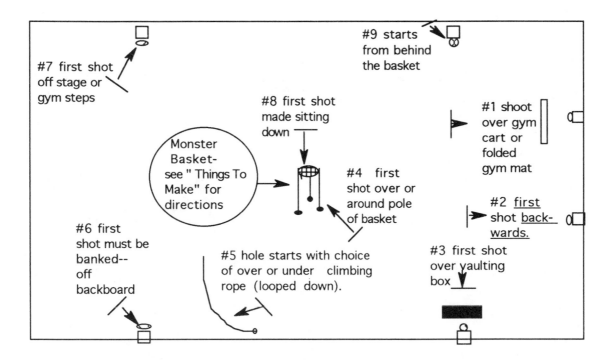

Suggestions:

❏ So that no one has a "disaster hole," set a maximum number of shots; for example, no one scores higher than seven on any one hole.

❏ Remind all students not to interfere with any ball rolling or bouncing across the gym.

Variations:

❏ For older students, enforce a "shoot it from where you catch it" rule; that is, if the ball is caught facing away from the basket, either shoot a hook shot, overhead backwards, or a turnaround jump shot.

❐ Don't have many baskets? Try barrel shots, using any type trash barrel. Examples: #1—Shot must be *bounced* into barrel to score. Place barrel about ten feet from shooting line. The ball may be bounced off the wall or floor. #2—Move barrel a few feet away from wall; ball must be banked off the wall into the barrel. NOTE: You might want to put a weight of some sort in the barrel to keep it from tipping over.

5.2 JUMP BALL

Grade Level: K-8

Description: A station for two to seven people that is *very* active.

Objective: This station will help develop jumping skills, especially the ability to "time" the jump and will also develop "blockout" skills as used in basketball.

Equipment: 1 tetherball; a long cord

Directions:

1. Tie a tetherball to a long piece of strong cord.

2. Suspend the tetherball from a ceiling beam or outside on a high tree branch. Toss the ball over the beam or branch.

3. Tie off the cord to a strong support. Set the ball high enough so that it is just above the outstretched fingers of the tallest player in the group.

4. Players try to jump and hit the ball. They will naturally try to block out others as they position themselves to hit the ball.

Suggestions:

❐ *Allow open hand hits only!*

❐ Caution students to hit the ball, not each other.

Variation: Make a game of this activity by having players call out their scores as they hit. The first player to get five hits is the winner. It helps if all players are approximately the same height, but this is not absolutely necessary.

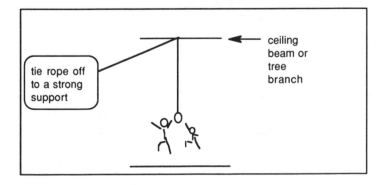

5.3 KICK 'N HIT

Grade Level: K-8

Description: A station to challenge visual memory and coordination. This looks similar to a karate practice, but it is good for visual training and for developing strength.

Objective: To keep both objects moving as long as possible using the hands and feet.

Equipment: 1 tetherball on a long cord, one large hanging object (either a small cage ball suspended on a rope or a low-hung punching bag—see Section 7).

Directions:

1. From one side of a basketball support, hang the tetherball down to about the head level of most students. Hang it toward the front of the basketball support so it's away from the wall. Tie off this tetherball rope to a door or other strong support.

2. Hang the large object from the other side of the basketball support. Tie off the rope so this object is suspended to just above the floor.

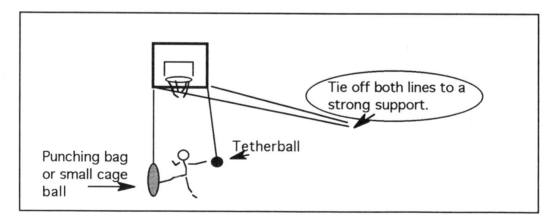

3. The student stands between the two objects facing away from the wall. He or she will attempt to hit (with the hand) the tetherball, and kick the larger object, keeping both objects going as long as possible.

Suggestions:

- ❏ Advanced players can attempt spin moves (as in karate) as they attempt to keep the objects moving.

- ❏ If the ball cords get tangled, allow them to untangle, and then continue.

- ❏ This is a station for a fitness unit, combat games station, or as part of a variety station set-up.

- ❏ One player at a time is at this station.

5.4 POP-UPS

Grade Level: 1-8

Description: When it's time to work on catching pop-ups, we often find that kids have trouble hitting the ball to one another, or if the teacher hits the pop-ups, kids just don't get enough turns catching. So here's a way for even first graders to hit pop-ups to each other.

Objective: To practice catching pop-ups as a station.

Equipment: Gloves are *not* needed; a tennis racquet; a whiffle ball

Directions:

1. Supply one racquet and one ball for each group. Four to five students per group work well.

2. Explain that the leader is to use the tennis racquet to swing underhand and hit pop-ups to the group.

Suggestions:

❐ Make this a contest. The first fielder to catch three pop-ups becomes the new batter; or allow each batter five hits, then switch batters.

❐ If kids are too aggressive fielding the pop-ups, have the batter call the name of the person who will field the catch.

Variation: With older students, you might switch to using a tennis ball for longer/higher fly balls.

5.5 RACKETBALL

Grade Level: 3-8

Description: Here's a way for young children to experience the great lifetime activity of racketball. It is used as a station.

Objective: To score points, as in regular racketball, but on a modified three-wall court.

Equipment: 2 walls and an improvised wall; 1 high-bounce Nerf™ tennis ball; 2 paddles (just about any type will do)

Directions:

1. Use a corner of the gym for the front and side walls, then add an improvised wall as described here.

For the improvised wall, use any of the following:	Support the wall with:

1. A table tennis top   about
2. A large crash pad   5' × 9'
3. A piece of plywood
    or anything that is
    reasonably smooth and flat
	1. Parallel bars
	2. A chair rack
	3. An equipment cart
	4. A vaulting box
	    or anything that will support the "wall"

2. Lean the improvised wall against a support. The wall doesn't have to be the full length of the side wall. The long side of the wall goes on the floor.

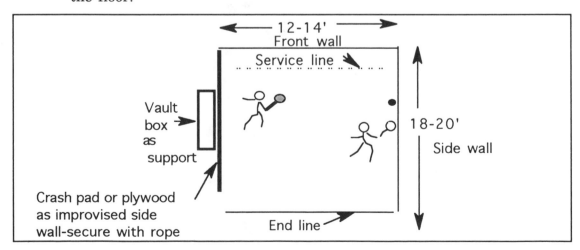

3. Explain the **rules:**
   a. The ball is served *underhand*—it must rebound back past the service line before hitting the floor. The serve can hit a side wall after hitting the front wall.
   b. Players alternate hitting the ball. They may hit the ball out of the air or after one bounce.
   c. Players lose points if they: allow the ball to bounce twice before hitting, do not hit the ball to the front wall before the ball hits the floor, do not return a ball that their opponent hits onto the court, or hit a ball that goes out of bounds.

Suggestions:

❒ Use as a station with other racket sports like ping-pong, floor pong, Goodminton, etc.

❒ Discuss the term/rule of "Hinder." A Hinder is called by a player who feels that he or she was blocked from getting to a ball or that it was unsafe to swing at the ball. The point is replayed.

❒ This game can also be played as handball with a large plastic ball or large super Nerf™ ball. No paddles are needed.

HOT-WEATHER STATIONS

When the weather becomes too hot for active play, it's time to set up some less active stations. These tend to be skill-oriented activities. They can be set up in shaded areas for increased comfort.

ACTIVITY INDICATOR

○	Less active
◍	Active
●	Very active
Ⓢ	Strength

6.1 FISHING

Grade Level: K-5

Description: A hot-weather station that's a great test of eye-hand coordination.

Objective: To "hook" and pull out "fish" from the "pond."

Equipment: A bucket or box; whiffle balls; a pole, string, and hook

Directions:

1. Tie a 2- to 3-foot piece of string onto one end of a 1½- to 3-foot length of wooden dowel rod.

2. To the other end of the string, attach a hook. The clip that comes with a whistle lanyard makes a safe hook. Tape the clip so that it stays fully open. Other types of hooks will also work. Just make sure they will fit into a whiffle ball hole and are safe—no sharp edges.

3. Fill a bucket with whiffle balls—color the balls, if you like, so you can have imaginary yellow perch, bluefish, red snapper, etc.

4. Students attempt to lower the hook into a whiffle ball hole, hook the "fish," and pull it out of the box.

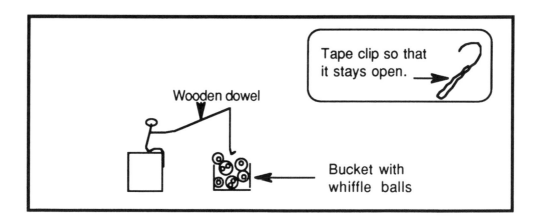

Suggestions:

❑ No more than two fishermen per pond.

❐ Use this activity as either a hot-weather sport station or a side activity for students who are eliminated from a game for whatever reason (sickness, injury, etc.).

❐ Attach points to different colors or sizes of balls, so fishermen can keep score.

❐ *Speed Fishing*—How many fish/points can you get in five minutes?

6.2 HOCKEY CROQUET

Grade Level: 1-8

Description: A favorite summertime game that just happens to be a good eye-hand coordination activity. This version uses indoor hockey equipment and can be played outside on the grass or in the gym.

Objective: To complete the croquet course with as few turns as possible.

Equipment: 1 plastic (or wooden) hockey stick for each player; 1 whiffle ball (plastic balls without holes also work) for each player; traffic cones

Directions:

1. Set up the course using cones to make the croquet "wickets" as shown.

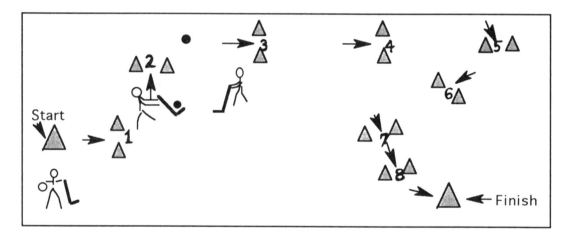

2. Color or mark the balls so each player knows which ball is his or hers.

3. Distribute one ball and one stick to each player (two to six players per game).

4. Explain the **rules:**

   a. Players take turns in order. Players normally get one hit per turn unless they hit another player's ball or go through a wicket. For each wicket and/or ball hit, they are awarded an extra hit. Players must go through wickets in the correct direction to earn extra hits. More than one extra hit can be earned on one shot.

b. If a ball stops between two cones, lay the stick across the top of the two cones to determine if the ball has gone through.

c. Play is started with a player placing his or her ball the length of the stick head away from the first cone to take his or her first shot.

d. The first player to complete the course is the winner. NOTE: It is often not an advantage going first as later players can earn extra shots by hitting the first player's ball.

Suggestions:

❏ Set up the course so that it challenges students. To make it more difficult, move a set of cones farther from the next set and/or position the cones that make up a wicket closer together.

❏ A circular course can be set up so that the starting line is also the finish line.

❏ Another variation is to have players retrace the course after hitting the finish cone, ending up at the starting cone.

❏ To play this game indoors on the floor, use hockey pucks instead of balls.

6.3 SOCK DARTS

Grade Level: K-8

Description: A hot-weather station that's easy to make and safe to play; a safe version of lawn darts.

Objective: To outscore your opponent by throwing your sock darts closer to the hoop or inside the hoop.

Equipment: 4 long tube-type socks (try to find socks with color identification on them—otherwise, color or dye to designate two sock darts of each color); filling material for socks (sand, beans, etc.); 2 hula hoops per game

Directions:

1. As with sock balls, put sand or beans into the toe of the sock to make a softball- or smaller-sized end. Tie off or wrap a rubber band around the end to contain the material.

2. Place hoops on the grass or court about eight to ten yards apart as shown.

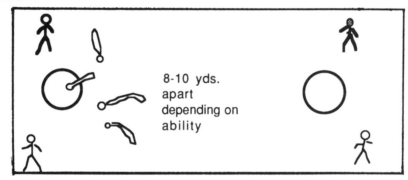

8-10 yds.
apart
depending on
ability

3. Two students stand to the side of one hoop. Players take turns throwing sock darts (best thrown by holding the open sock end and swinging underhand). The bean or sand filled end is the *scoring end.* If playing *doubles,* teammates stand at opposite hoops. (See the illustration.) They stand to the side to avoid being hit and interfering with play.

4. *Scoring:* Three points are awarded for a "ringer"—inside the hoop. Otherwise, one point is scored for each dart closer than your opponent's. Only one team or player scores. In the illustration, the white team scores three points, the black team none. If the black team had two darts closer than the white team's first dart, it would score two points.

6.4 TARGET BALL

Grade Level: K-8

Description: A hot-weather target activity with many variations. It is played outside on the field.

Objective: To position your ball (or other object) closer to the target than your opponent does.

Equipment: 1 Frisbee™ per game; 1 tennis ball per player (see variations below)

Directions:

1. Distribute the Frisbee™ and tennis balls to the group.
2. Explain the procedure:
   a. One player throws the Frisbee™ onto the playing area.
   b. Each player then throws a ball, attempting to get the ball as close as possible to the target object (the Frisbee™).
   c. The player whose ball is closest wins and gets to throw the target onto the field for the next point. Throws may be made far away or close; it's the thrower's choice.

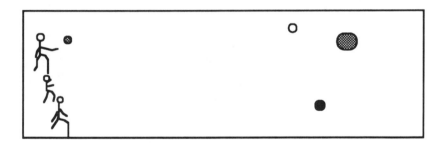

Suggestion:

❏ Let the whole class play in groups of three to five or use as a hot weather station.

Variations: These are endless. Some possible combinations are:

- ☐ Softballs and a football
- ☐ Lacrosse sticks and balls thrown toward a Frisbee™
- ☐ Frisbees™ as target **and** throwing objects
- ☐ Meteor balls (see Section 7) thrown at a target
- ☐ Footballs kicked toward a target ball or Frisbee™

THINGS TO MAKE

If you like to recycle, if you like to save money, if you like to make unique equipment for your program, try some of these projects. No special skills are required. Be prepared to make small modifications from the given directions to suit your particular equipment and circumstances. Have fun creating!

ACTIVITY INDICATOR

○	Less active
◍	Active
●	Very active
Ⓢ	Strength

7.1 BADMINTON BIRD DISPENSER

Description: An easy-to-make badminton bird holder that protects the birds, recycles old tennis ball containers, and is fun to use. It holds about ten birds.

Equipment: 1 discarded tennis ball container (clear plastic is best so that the birds are visible); 1 small piece of cord; 1 tennis can lid; badminton birds

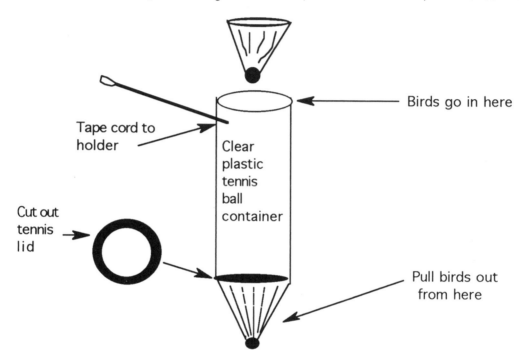

Birds go in here

Tape cord to holder

Clear plastic tennis ball container

Cut out tennis lid

Pull birds out from here

Color the ends of birds for greater visibility--Container holds about 10 birds

Directions:

1. Saw (or use a pen knife) to remove the bottom of the plastic tennis ball container. Sand edges smooth or tape, as this will be the *top* of the holder.

2. Tape a piece of cord or string to the top so you can hang the holder.

3. Cut a circle out of the tennis ball lid (a pen knife or X-acto™ knife will work). Make this hole just big enough so the birds will go only about ¾ of the way through the hole, but will not fall out. Attach this lid to the bottom of the tennis ball holder.

4. Drop birds into the top of the holder. Pull out from the bottom.

7.2 BATTING STATION

Description: Kids never seem to tire of this station. They can hit as hard as they like, as often as they like, with no worry about hitting anyone. It can be set up indoors between two baskets (as shown) or outside between two trees or poles.

Objective: To provide the opportunity for unlimited batting practice without the necessity of chasing the ball, setting the ball on a "T," or needing a pitcher.

Equipment: 2 whiffle balls; strong cord; 1 bat per ball (the new styrofoam barrel bats work best, but plastic bats are also good); nylon line

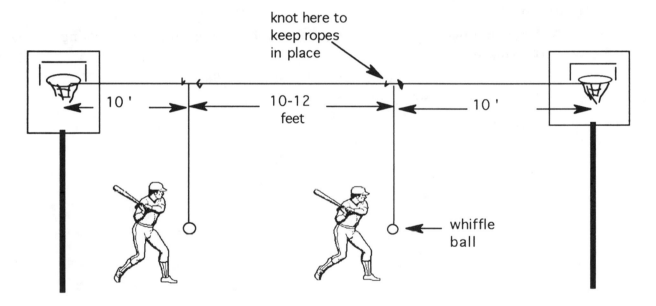

Directions:

1. String a horizontal line between the baskets or trees that you plan to use.

2. Hang a whiffle ball on a piece of nylon line (parachute cord). Thread cord through two whiffle ball holes and tie to main cord. (See the illustration.)

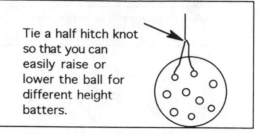

Tie a half hitch knot so that you can easily raise or lower the ball for different height batters.

3. At the top of this line, make another *small* loop that goes over the horizontal line. (Or, for a smoother operation, tie the cord to a small circular key ring—whistle lanyards usually have these.) When both vertical lines are in place (about 10 to 12 feet apart), tie a knot on either side of the whiffle ball line to keep it in place. If hung properly, the ball, when hit, will swing easily and often will swing completely around the horizontal line.

Variations:

❐ Batters have the option of stopping the ball before hitting or hitting a moving ball.

❐ Use as a batting station or with students who are having difficulty with batting skills.

7.3 CHAIR RACK EQUIPMENT CART

Description: A sports carry-all that recycles old chair racks.

Objective: To inexpensively utilize a chair rack as "the best ever" equipment cart. You'll wonder how you ever got along without one. I made my first one in 1980. Each year I add something to it.

Equipment: A chair rack; assorted pieces of plywood; dowel rod; pieces of cord

Directions:

1. Obtain a chair rack. Call the warehouse that stores unused equipment or locate one from another source. Usually they are glad to find a use for these relics.

2. Cut out a piece of plywood that will fit into the bottom of the cart.

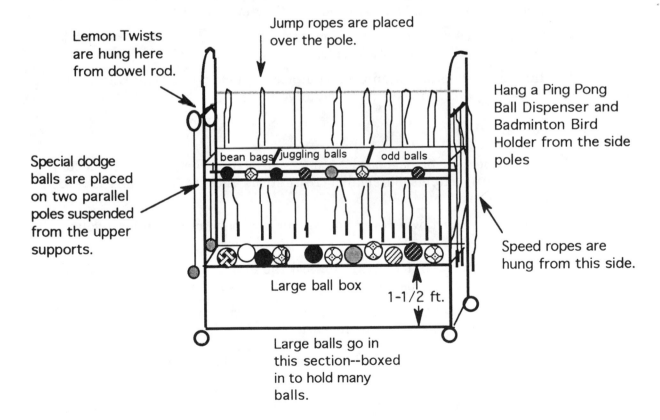

Lemon Twists are hung here from dowel rod.

Jump ropes are placed over the pole.

Hang a Ping Pong Ball Dispenser and Badminton Bird Holder from the side poles

Special dodge balls are placed on two parallel poles suspended from the upper supports.

bean bags juggling balls odd balls

Large ball box

Speed ropes are hung from this side.

1-1/2 ft.

Large balls go in this section--boxed in to hold many balls.

3. Box in this bottom section with plywood (about 1½ feet wide) so that it will hold a variety of balls that are used in your program.

4. Just below the upper shelf of the chair rack, suspend two parallel poles about six to eight inches apart. Tape these poles so as to maintain the correct distance apart. Your favorite dodge balls will be stored here.

5. On the upper section of the chair rack itself, place a piece of plywood covering the entire shelf. Then border all the way around with a 2 inch wide plywood strip to form a box. Divide this shelf into three sections: one for juggling balls, one for beanbags, one for miscellaneous balls, or use one section for paddles.

6. Tie a piece of dowel rod (or an old broomstick handle) to one side of the cart for jump ropes. Place this high enough so that the ropes will not touch the floor. This pole will easily hold 50 jump ropes.

7. Fasten small sections of dowel rod at both ends of the cart. These should span the two main vertical supports of the cart. From one, hang your vinyl jump ropes or speed ropes. On the other, place hooks from which to hang Lemon Twists.

8. Hang a Ping-Pong Ball Holder from one pole and a Badminton Bird Holder from the other pole. (See the directions in this section.)

9. You might be able to place one more shelf at the top of the chair rack for storing stilts, pogo sticks, etc.

10. Hang or store other often-used equipment, such as juggling rings, soft Frisbees™, etc., on the cart in creative ways.

Suggestions:

❐ Hang a section of pegboard on one side of the cart. This allows for hanging single items like small lacrosse sticks, rackets, Trac Ball rackets, soft Frisbees™, etc.

❐ Roll out the cart whenever you're working on jump rope or juggling skills.

❐ Occasionally roll out the cart toward the end of the gym period for a "free time" session using the equipment on the cart.

❐ Teach students how to use the equipment correctly and to return it to the appropriate location on the cart.

7.4 FINGER WHISTLE

Description: A whistle is often needed for quick response and for safety. But there are several reasons why wearing a whistle around the neck is unappealing to many. This easy modification allows a whistle to be inconspicuous, readily at hand, and out of the way when demonstrating. It is held in the palm of the hand when it is needed quickly, but is flipped over to the back of the hand when demonstrating.

Objective: To inexpensively transform an ordinary plastic whistle into a finger whistle.

Equipment: 1 plastic whistle; 1 three- to four-inch piece of ¼-inch (or ½-inch) elastic band

Directions:

1. Wrap the elastic material around the finger you will use (usually one of the middle fingers). Overlap the material about ½ inch. Mark this spot and cut the elastic.
2. Thread the elastic through the metal ring that is attached to the whistle. Again, overlap the elastic material.
3. Sew the elastic together so that you have one circle of material.

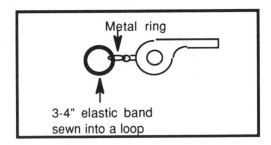

Variation: If you want the whistle closer to your finger, try the following:

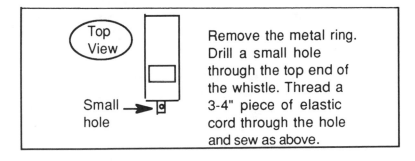

7.5 FOUR-WAY TUG-O-WAR

Grade Level: 1-8

Description: A strength-building activity that's a bit different and much fun.

Objective: Be the first player to pick up a beanbag while holding onto the tug rope.

Equipment: 2 seven-foot sections of strong rope; 4 eight- to ten-inch sections of garden hose; 4 beanbags.

Directions:

1. Knot two pieces of strong rope together at their centers (strong *jump rope* works, but *mountain climbing rope* is best). Knot the ropes tightly so there is no slippage.

2. At each of the four ends, form a loop for a handle (about eight inches in diameter should do it). Slide a piece of garden hose over this, then knot the end of the rope to the main line as shown. A bowline knot works best here.

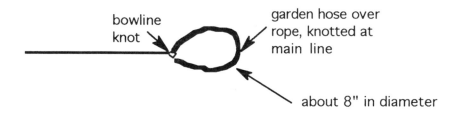

bowline knot

garden hose over rope, knotted at main line

about 8" in diameter

3. Stretch the 4-way rope out on the floor.

4. Place a bean-bag out of reach of each participant. Mark spots on the floor so the bean-bags can be returned to the same spot. Use a permanent magic marker to draw on the floor the exact placement of the four-way rope.

5. *Rules:* Only one—**Do not ever let go in a tug activity!** If a participant feels he or she cannot hold on, he or she should shout "Stop."

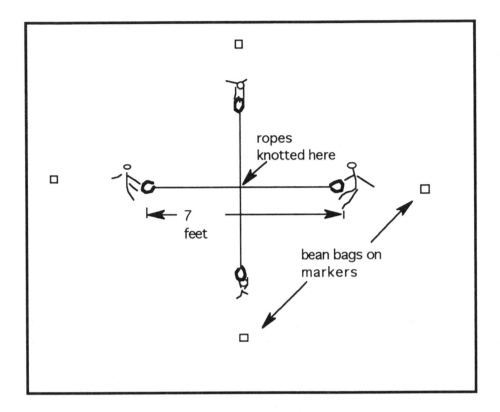

ropes
knotted here

7
feet

bean bags on
markers

Suggestion:

❒ Be sure the beanbags are placed far enough from any obstacles in case
someone slips. Everyone will be pulling hard!

Variations:

❒ Have participants sit on the floor and put one foot through the loop.
Using hands on the floor, attempt to reach the bag. This is a great
exercise for stomach and arms.

❒ Use for partner tug—two against two in a normal tug-o-war.

7.6 HANDSTAND/PUSH-UP BARS

Description: A homemade set of bars that allows for easier headstands and handstands and more challenging push-ups.

Equipment: 1½-inch PVC pipe and connecting pieces (this is a good way to use those small sections of leftover PVC pipe)

Directions:

1. Cut pipe to the following dimensions for *two* bars:
   - 2 pieces—10½ inches long
   - 4 pieces—2½ inches long
   - 4 pieces—3¼ inches long
   - 4 pieces—1¾ inches long
   - 4—90-degree elbow sections
   - 4—T-joints
   - PVC cement

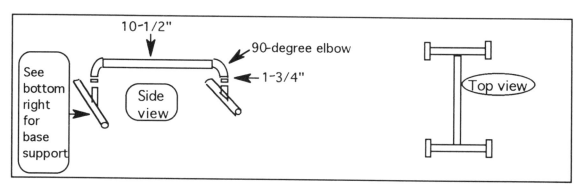

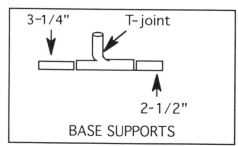

BASE SUPPORTS

2. Glue a 2½-inch piece to the long end of a T-joint and a 3¼-inch piece to the short end of the same T-joint (see base support illustration). Repeat for the other base section.

3. Glue the 1¾-inch pieces into the top of the T-joints.

4. Glue the 10½-inch pieces to the 90-degree elbows, making sure the elbows are symmetrical. Lay pieces flat on the floor to get them even.

5. Glue the base supports to the bar sections to complete.

Suggestion:

❏ For a more professional final product, add a coupling piece to the ends of each base support section.

7.7 HAMMER THROW

Description: A modified throwing implement, very similar to the real event, to add to your track-and-field unit.

Objective: To inexpensively and safely have children experience this unique throwing event.

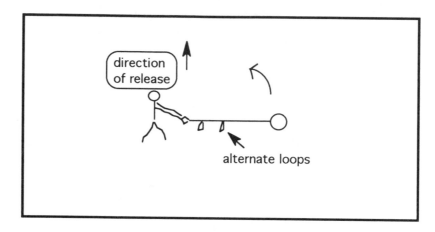

Equipment: 1 tetherball; 6-8 feet of strong cord

Directions:

1. Attach a strong cord to the tetherball if one is not already attached.

2. Knot the cord in several places to form loops. This provides loops of varying distances from the ball. Students can choose the loop that suits them best. Either a "bowline" knot or "half hitch" knot provides a non-slip loop.

3. Explain *how to throw:* Stand sideways to the intended direction of travel. Swing the ball in a circle in a slightly upward arc in front of the body. The cord loop may be held with one or both hands. Spin the ball around the body to gain speed, then release on a forward swing. Additional force can be obtained by stepping forward as the throw is made.

Suggestion:

❐ Caution students to stay away from the thrower, as well as the intended landing area. As a precaution, *cone off the area.* Have the thrower chase his or her own throw so that no one is in the throwing area at the time of the throw.

7.8 HANDWEIGHTS MADE SAFE

(S)

Description: A way to make small hand weights (dumbbells) safer to use. If you like to teach children the correct way to use handweights, but worry about accidents, try this easy solution.

Objective: To make a desirable activity safer for children.

Equipment: Small dumbbells (3 to 5 pounds); tennis balls

Directions:

1. Cut out a circle in the side of the tennis ball just big enough so it will fit over the dumbbell ends. Cut this hole with a penknife or X-acto™ blade. Start with a small hole—enlarge until you get a snug fit.

2. Cut another circle out of a second tennis ball for the other half of the dumbbell.

3. Slip both tennis ball pieces over the dumbbell ends. (See the illustration.) Just this small amount of cushioning makes a great deal of difference in the event of a mishap.

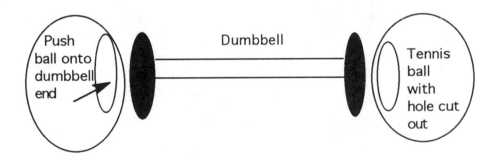

7.9 PVC HURDLES

Description: A reasonable alternative to commercially bought hurdles. These hurdles are inexpensive, durable, and easy to transport.

Objective: To provide reasonably priced, lightweight hurdles. The following directions are for a 24-inch high hurdle that can also serve as a 13-inch high hurdle for younger children.

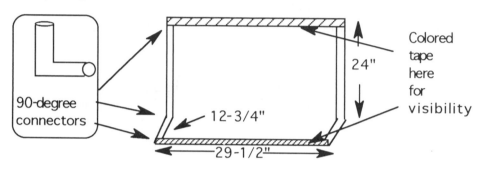

Equipment: ¾-inch PVC pipe (available in most hardware stores); PVC cement; colorful tape

Directions:

1. Cut ¾-inch PVC pipe to the above dimensions. Smooth any rough edges from the cut ends. Assemble without cement first.

2. After sections of the hurdle have been cut and laid out for assembly, use *PVC cement* to permanently bond the pipes. Make sure the 90-degree elbow joints are positioned correctly. Glue bottom section first.

3. Put colorful tape on the top and bottom pieces for visibility.

Suggestions:

❐ If a *lower hurdle* is desired for grades 1 or 2, place the 24-inch section on the floor; you then have a 13-inch high hurdle.

❐ Teach students to *always* jump toward the colored portion of the hurdle. It's the correct direction and safer for both the hurdler and the hurdle.

❐ Try a Shuttle Hurdle Relay. Start the race from one direction. All participants will hurdle going in the hurdle direction, then when it's their turn to go again, sprint *between* the hurdles in the other direction.

Each runner will tag the waiting teammate who runs back again. Have runners sit down after their second turn. Extra people will be needed to right any hurdle that has been knocked over.

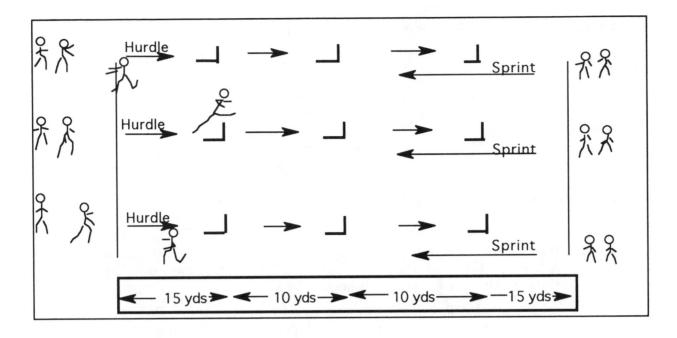

7.10 JAVELIN MADE SAFE

Description: A safe version of the javelin.

Objective: To give students the experience of throwing a modified version of a javelin. It gives the experience of participating in this standard field event without the potential danger of using an actual javelin.

Equipment: Tennis ball; 48-inch section of dowel rod (¼-inch diameter); 48-inch section of ½-inch plastic tubing for sliding over dowel (get this at a hardware store—usually sold in bulk rolls); tape; colorful ribbon or scarf

Directions:

1. Cut a small slit in the tennis ball (about ½ inch or so).

2. Wrap a small piece of tape around the end of the wooden dowel to keep it from cutting into the tennis ball, and insert the dowel into the ball. Enlarge the cut if needed; it should be snug.

3. Slide the plastic tubing over the dowel and into the tennis ball. The tubing provides a nice surface to hold. The dowel gives the javelin rigidity. The tennis ball will stay in place unless pulled away forcefully.

4. Secure the tubing by gluing or stapling it to the dowel; tape over any staples. Some tape at the balance point shows students where to hold the javelin.

5. Add a colorful ribbon or scarf to the end for decorative purposes and better flight, and your students are ready to throw.

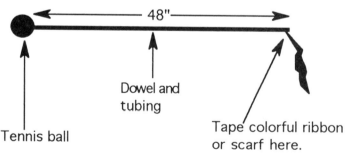

48"

Tennis ball

Dowel and tubing

Tape colorful ribbon or scarf here.

Suggestions:

❏ The secret to throwing a javelin is to keep it straight in line when preparing to throw; do not twist the javelin sideways. When thrown, the weight of the tennis ball brings down the "point" first.

❏ Use as a station in track and field or as a sports-day event.

Variation:

❏ Use any light tubing that seems appropriate for making a javelin. I recently made one out of a "rope on a stick" (a jump rope that is attached to the two ends of a wand and is jumped by holding the wand). It was 35 inches long and ¾ inch in diameter. All I had to do was add the tennis ball and scarf—it even had a hand grip!

7.11 JUGGLING BALLS

Description: Juggling equipment to add excitement to your program that's inexpensive to make.

Objective: To motivate students to achieve success in the difficult skill of juggling, and to make juggling equipment inexpensively for your program and/or your students.

Equipment: 3 tennis balls; fabric dye; an empty tennis ball can

Directions:

1. Acquire used tennis balls from your community—these make fine juggling balls.

2. Dye 50-60 tennis balls at a time in a large bucket or trash barrel using a dark color fabric dye (red or blue works best). Do one dyeing for a red color and one for blue or black.

3. Use a tennis ball in its normal light green color to give you a third color. Dry all balls ***thoroughly.*** Package each set of three balls into a can with a lid.

4. Award a can of balls to each student passing your juggling requirement (mine is ten throws in the normal juggling pattern). You might want to further decorate the can by wrapping with a label that you've duplicated with cartoon jugglers, date of accomplishment, name, etc. (See Section 10 for a sample printout.)

5. ***Juggling Beanbag Balls***—See "Sock Balls" in this section for directions to make juggling bags.
   Tennis Ball Giveaway—To motivate young children to work on the juggling and other ball skills that you are practicing in class, why not have a tennis ball giveaway? Put a notice in your PTA bulletin asking for used tennis balls. Dye them if you wish, then give one to each of your first graders at the end of your throwing/catching unit. This is also a good way to recycle used tennis balls.

7.12 JUGGLING PINS

Description: Two types of juggling pins that are very inexpensive.

Objective: To make pins for juggling.

Equipment: (For each pin) 1 plastic quart size bleach bottle; 1 piece of ⅞-inch wooden dowel 16-17 inches long; 1 wood screw; tape to finish the project

Directions:

1. Drill a small starter hole in one end of the dowel.
2. Drill a small hole in the bottom end of the bleach bottle at the center.
3. Insert the wooden dowel section into the bleach bottle.
4. Use the screw to fasten the dowel permanently to the bottle.
5. Tape over the mouth of the bleach bottle to eliminate any looseness.

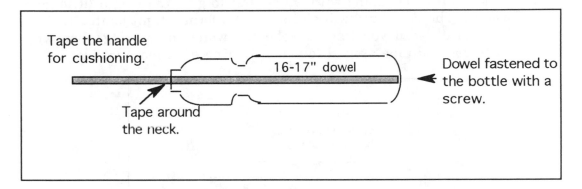

Variation: Make newspaper pins.

a. Lay out six full sheets of newspaper.
b. Cut off the top six inches of all sheets—set aside.
c. Roll up the sheets of newspaper into a tight roll—tape to secure.
d. Roll the 6-inch section tightly around the top of the main section. Tape in place.
e. Use athletic or other tape to tape over the entire pin.
f. Use colorful tape to add stripes of color.

7.13 JUGGLING RINGS

Description: Inexpensive rings for a variety of uses that are durable and won't hurt the hands when caught.

Equipment: ½-inch diameter flexible tubing; ⅜-inch wooden dowel; tape

Directions:

1. Buy some ½-inch diameter flexible plastic tubing from a hardware store (usually sold in bulk rolls).
2. Cut about a 2½-foot section (make larger or smaller if you like).
3. Cut about a one-inch section of ⅜-inch wooden dowel rod. Taper both ends of dowel slightly.
4. Then close the ring by placing the dowel rod into each end of tubing. Push together to close. (See the illustration.)
5. I like to fill the tubing with water first to give the ring a little more weight. The dowel rod will also swell and form a tight joint. Drop in a little food dye if you want to color the water in the ring, then wrap some colorful tape around to make the ring even more visible.

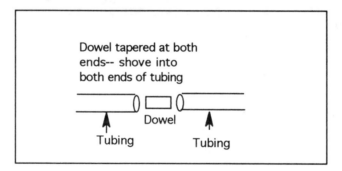

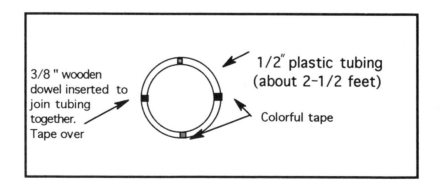

7.14 JUMP ROPE REPAIR

Description: Vinyl jump ropes sometimes break. Don't throw them away. Use sections of the vinyl material to repair balls (see "Plastic Volleyball Repair" in this section) or repair the rope itself. With this procedure you also have the option of making the repaired rope whatever length you want.

Objective: To repair broken vinyl jump ropes.

Equipment: Monofilament (fishing line); tape

Directions:

1. Drill a small hole through each end of the jump rope pieces to be joined together. Use an electic drill and your smallest drill bit.

2. Thread a small piece of monofilament (fishing line) through both the holes and tie tightly. Then wrap some tape around the repaired section to completely cover the monofilament. This keeps the monofilament from coming untied. That's it! Now you have a useable jump rope again.

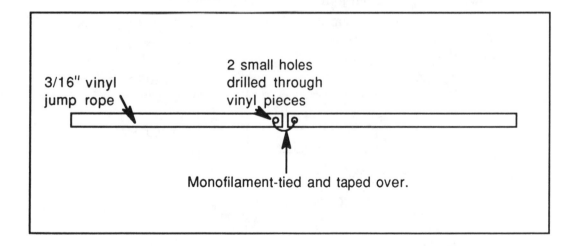

Section Seven / THINGS TO MAKE

7.15 PVC LACROSSE GOALS

Description: Easy-to-make goals that can be used for lacrosse, floor hockey, and team handball. The advantages: they are relatively inexpensive (about $20 each) and light enough that kids can transport.

Objective: To make inexpensive goals for a variety of uses.

Equipment: 1½-inch PVC pipe, available at good hardware stores (you can cover these with any netting, but purchasing regular lacrosse goal netting adds a nice touch); PVC cement

Directions:

1. Purchase the amount of pipe needed (three 10-foot sections will give you more than enough) plus three 90-degree joints and two T-joints for each goal. PVC cement is also needed.
2. Cut sections to the required dimensions, as shown.
3. Be sure to remove any rough edges from the cut ends with a knife.
4. Glue the two 3' 11" pieces to a 90-degree joint with PVC cement.
5. Glue the two 5' 2" side pieces to the 5' 10" top piece using the two remaining 90-degree joints.
6. Assemble the rest of the goal together, but don't glue yet.
7. Now take apart each joint not yet glued, and glue with PVC cement.
8. When the goal is assembled, paint to distinguish, or just run a piece of colored tape down the front sections of the goal.

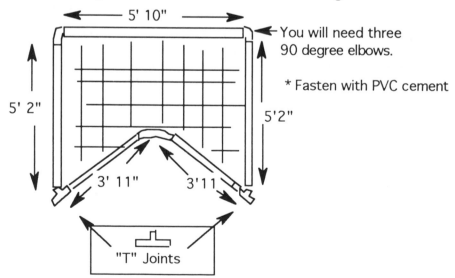

Suggestions:

❐ Another use I've found for these goals: they are a nice way to block an outside gym door to keep balls from flying out, while letting cool air in.

❐ These goals can be made even more durable by putting a brace piece of PVC pipe running from the back bottom elbow joint to the middle of the top piece of pipe. Bolt brace to the main goal.

7.16 PVC Lacrosse Mini-Goals

Description: Lightweight goals that can be used in a number of games or as targets.

Objective: These goals are easier to store than the full sized goals; they are good for small group indoor games and a modified (no goalie) lacrosse game outside. Also, if you provide students with the directions for making these, backyard lacrosse games will begin to pop up in your neighborhood.

Equipment: 12½ feet of 1¼-inch PVC pipe, available at most hardware stores; 5 90-degree elbow joints (also 1¼-inch pipe); PVC cement

Directions:

1. Cut pipe with a saw to the sizes shown.
2. Clean ends of the cut pipe with a knife to eliminate ragged edges.
3. Glue together the bottom section first. To make the goal a little more stable, you might want to wedge or tape some sort of weight into the back bottom joint.
4. Glue in the side sections of the goal so they are perpendicular.
5. Glue in the top section.
6. Use any netting to cover the goal (tape netting to goal); color with tape, or paint first if desired.

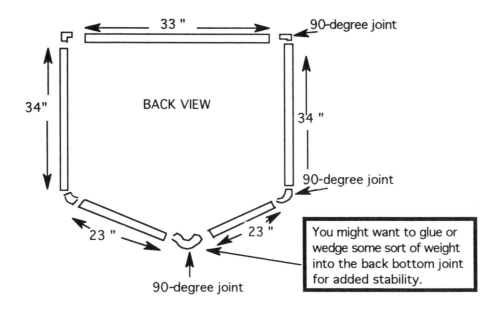

7.17 LEMON TWIST

Description: This is an individual activity that combines jogging and jumping. These are so inexpensive and so easy to make that you can make enough for a whole class activity, or give them to classes to use during recess. They can also be a do-it-yourself project for participants.

Objective: To jump the tennis ball as it swings around the jumper's foot.

Equipment: (For each Lemon Twist) 38-40" length of nylon cord; 10-11" length of nylon cord; 15-16" section of ½-inch flexible plastic tubing (sold in bulk rolls at hardware stores); 1 large lace lock (sold in outdoor supply stores or athletic stores); 1 tennis ball

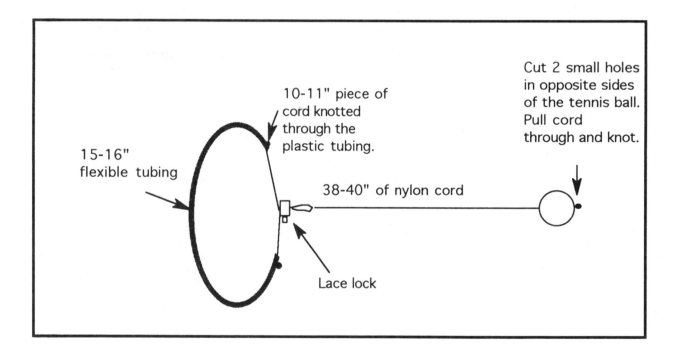

Cut 2 small holes in opposite sides of the tennis ball. Pull cord through and knot.

10-11" piece of cord knotted through the plastic tubing.

15-16" flexible tubing

38-40" of nylon cord

Lace lock

Directions:

1. Drill a small hole about ½ inch from both ends of the plastic tubing.

2. Insert the ends of the 10-11" piece of cord through the holes and knot. Push the middle of this cord through the lace lock (or use the hook tool to pull the cord through). Tie the long piece of cord to this loop.

3. Cut two small (½-inch) slits in opposite sides of the tennis ball.

4. Pull the long cord through the holes you've cut into the tennis ball. To do this, make a hook tool by bending the end of a coat hanger into a narrow hook; push the hook through both holes, hook the cord, and pull back through the ball.

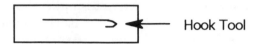
Hook Tool

5. *How to Use:* Place the Lemon Twist loop over the good foot (kicking foot). Squeeze the lace lock and pull the cord to close the plastic tubing loop. Hold the cord near the ball in the good hand. Swing the ball forward in a circle. Then step/jog, step/jog, keeping the ball swinging. To remove from foot, squeeze lace lock to open loop.

Variations:

❐ Have students try dribbling another ball after they get the Lemon Twist swinging.

❐ Older children can try to juggle *and* Lemon Twist simultaneously.

7.18 LONG JUMP MAT

(S)

Description: It's so easy to make a standard tumbling mat into a testing mat for the long jump.

Objective: To make a measuring device for use in the standing long jump.

Equipment: 1 flat mat (folding mats don't work as well); yard stick; magic marker

Directions:

1. Place a yard stick even with one edge of the mat. Make a small mark on the mat using magic marker every inch, beginning at two feet.

2. When marks have been made up to seven feet (or 8 feet for older students), darken the marks so that it looks something like this:

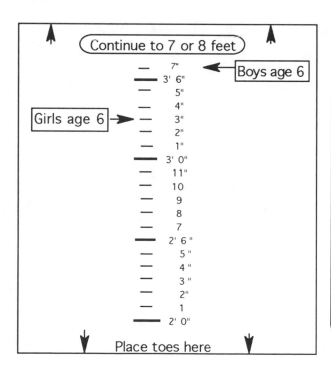

Alongside the appropriate distance indicate the age group norms--boys norms on one side, girls on the other, as shown at left. *Other norms can be found in the Ready To Use section under Fitness Test.

3. When using the long jump mat, place it near a wall with a soft object (like a folded tumbling mat) against the wall to extend the long jump mat farther from the wall as shown.

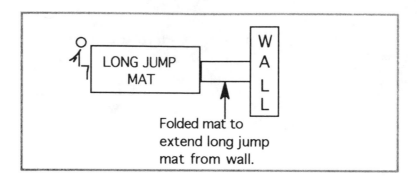

Folded mat to extend long jump mat from wall.

7.19 MEDICINE BALL

Description: An inexpensive medicine ball that's easy to make and, at virtually no cost, adds another piece of fitness equipment to your program.

Objective: To make a piece of equipment to develop upper body strength.

Equipment: A discarded leather ball (soccer or volleyball) that has stitched seams; some filler material (Use pieces of rubber, old jerseys, etc.; anything that has some weight, but is not too hard. Vary the type of filler to get the weight ball you want. Put heavier material in the center of the ball. My medicine ball weighs about 4 pounds and has been in use for over ten years.); strong thread and needle

Directions:

1. Cut open one panel of the ball at the seam.

2. Stuff filler material inside until you are happy with the weight and shape.

3. Sew the seam with strong thread.

Suggestions:

❑ Allow throwing with two hands only—no dodge-type throws.

❑ The ball can be thrown underhand to oneself or passed with a basketball-like chest pass to one or more partners.

❑ Use as a station for 2 or more people.

7.20 MONSTER BASKET

Description: A large shooting basket that's inexpensive and easy to make.

Objective: To enable *all* children, regardless of age or ability, to experience the fun of shooting a basket.

Equipment: If you are fortunate to have available three portable volleyball standards, you can easily make a "Monster Basket." Also needed are a hula hoop (24-26"); a basketball net and some type of hooks (to make set-up and take-down easy); cord (bungee cord works best) NOTE: If only two volleyball standards are available, the third cord could be tied off to any sturdy object of the same height.

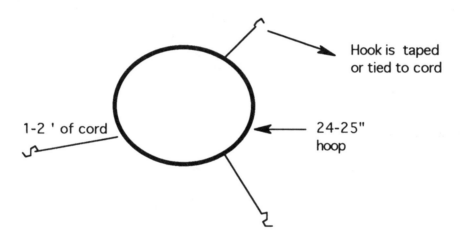

Hook is taped or tied to cord

1-2 ' of cord

24-25" hoop

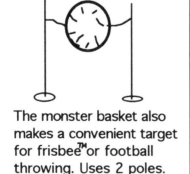

The monster basket also makes a convenient target for frisbee™or football throwing. Uses 2 poles.

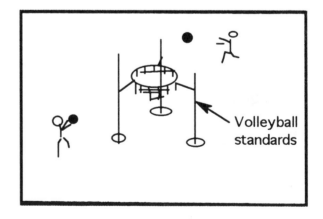

Volleyball standards

Directions:

1. Cut open the hoop so you can thread a standard basketball net onto it.

2. Then refasten the hoop. (Use a small piece of wooden dowel plugged into each end of the hoop—staple hoop to the dowel inside, then tape over.) Tape the top of the net to the hoop to keep it in place.

3. Attach three cords onto the hoop at three equally spaced locations and tie or tape a hook at the end of each cord.

4. Now attach the hooks to the eyelets of the volleyball poles at the height you want. You now have a super-large basket that can be raised or lowered by moving the three hooks to new eyelets.

5. My basket has been in service for well over ten years without *any* repairs! This is a *shooting* basket, but it is very sturdy. Though occasionally bumped, mine has never come close to falling over.

Variation:

☐ If there are not enough eyelets on the pole, or you don't have hooks, use three clothesline jump ropes to tie the basket to the poles.

7.21 METEOR BALL

Description: An inexpensive throwing implement that's easy to make and adds another eye-hand coordination activity to your program. A good hot-weather activity, but kids delight in throwing and chasing these no matter what the weather.

Objective: To make a throwing object to be used in several throwing/catching games.

Equipment: (For each Meteor Ball) 2 scarves (juggling scarves work just fine, but any lightweight scarf will work); 1 tennis ball; a hook tool (make a hook tool by bending the end of a coat hanger into narrow hook)

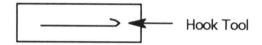
Hook Tool

Directions:

1. Cut two slits in the tennis ball (on opposite sides of the ball).
2. Push the hook tool through both slits.
3. Hook the scarf with the hook tool, then pull the hook tool back through the ball, pulling the scarf back through the ball.
4. Knot the scarf once or twice so it will not pull back through the ball.
5. Tie a second scarf to the end of the first. Use two different colored scarves for each ball.

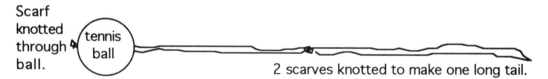
Scarf knotted through ball. tennis ball — 2 scarves knotted to make one long tail.

6. Meteor balls are thrown by the scarf end, by swinging in an underhand motion until ready to release toward the top of the swing. They are also caught by the tail. If you want to award points in a game the scoring is: one point for catching the very end of the scarf; two points for catching the middle knot; and three points for catching the scarf closer to the ball.

Variation:

❒ Use a piece of cord instead of scarves to make your Meteor Ball.

7.22 PEGBOARD SCOREBOARD

Description: A simple way to transform your pegboard into a highly visible and cost-free scoreboard. To be used for keeping score in any game such as box soccer, floor hockey, and others.

Equipment: A square pegboard that is not too high off the ground, unwanted softball or baseball bats; two colored tennis balls

Directions:

1. Cut two 5½-inch long sections from wooden bats at a thickness that will give a rather snug fit when the narrower end is inserted into the pegboard holes. Measure hole and bat to get the right thickness (about 3 cm usually).

2. Use a sharp knife to cut out a circular hole in the two tennis balls (one red or blue and one the standard yellow/green color). Insert the thicker end of each peg section into each tennis ball hole—this should be a snug fit so no glue or nails are necessary. Repeat with the other colored ball.

3. Mark the peg holes for scoring. Use tape or magic marker. The bottom two rows of holes are for one team's score and the next two rows above are for the opposing team.

4. Place a folded mat or something similar for students to stand on so they can reach the holes. First graders can reach the upper holes from a folded mat if the bottom of the pegboard is 5 to 5½ feet from the floor.

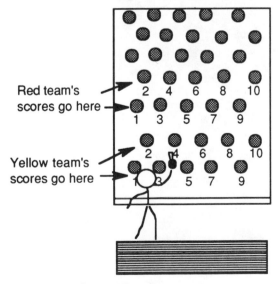
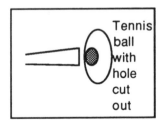

Suggestion:

❏ If your pegboard is in an area where the scorekeepers may be in the way of the game or create a safety hazard, barricade the scoreboard area with a folded mat stood on its side and placed in front of the scoreboard.

7.23 PING-PONG BALL DISPENSER/HOLDER

Description: A simple-to-make project that protects ping-pong balls and makes it fun for students to get and return balls.

Objective: To build a storage container for ping-pong balls.

Equipment: a length of 1½-inch PVC pipe—each foot of pipe will store about seven balls; 1 90-degree PVC elbow joint (also 1½ inch); a piece of cord; 3 tubeless tire plugs or sections of vinyl jump rope; PVC cement

Directions:

1. Cut the PVC pipe to the length you want (2-3 feet is adequate).
2. Use PVC cement to glue the elbow joint to the straight pipe end.
3. Use a saw to cut away a section of the elbow that's facing upward so that fingers can get to the ball (see illustration).
4. Drill three small holes into the elbow joint as shown. Insert tire repair plugs or vinyl jump rope material into these holes. These plugs stop the ball from rolling out. Cut off any excess. Glue in place if needed.
5. Attach the cord to the top of the holder, drop in balls, and hang in a convenient spot.

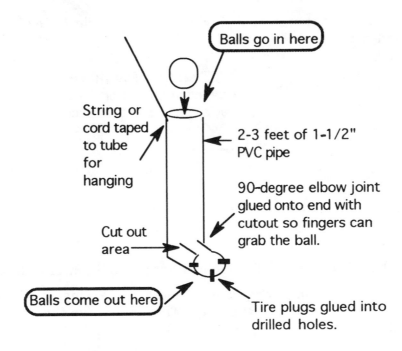

Balls go in here

String or cord taped to tube for hanging

2-3 feet of 1-1/2" PVC pipe

90-degree elbow joint glued onto end with cutout so fingers can grab the ball.

Cut out area

Balls come out here

Tire plugs glued into drilled holes.

7.24 PLASTIC BALL REPAIR

Description: Finally, a solution to the problem of deflated plastic balls. It's so simple and quick I wish I'd discovered it long ago. No longer do we have to throw out all those deflated balls, many of which have seen only one year's service.

Objective: To revive "dead" plastic balls, recycling not only them but broken jump ropes as well.

Equipment: Deflated plastic balls; a pump (electric pumps work best); vinyl jump rope pieces

Directions:

1. When plastic volleyballs have lost their air, don't throw them away, pump them back up! To do so, you will need to break the seal. Stick a regular pump needle into the ball, breaking the seal.

2. Cut about a ½-inch long section of **vinyl jump rope** (³⁄₁₆-inch diameter) or similar material.

3. Pump up the ball to the size you want. Pull out the needle and hold your finger over the hole.

4. Quickly insert the section of vinyl rope into the hole. Snip off any excess or sand down to make smooth.

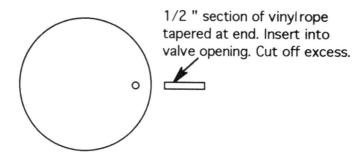

1/2 " section of vinyl rope tapered at end. Insert into valve opening. Cut off excess.

Suggestions:

☐ *If the hole is too small,* file the end of the vinyl material to taper.

☐ *If the hole is too big,* wrap a small piece of masking or adhesive tape around the top of the vinyl section. This will wedge the vinyl material into the hole.

7.25 PUNCHING BAG

Description: The trouble with many punching bags is they're too hard and hurt small hands. This alternative is soft enough that no gloves are needed, although gloves do add authenticity to the activity.

Objective: One of the most enjoyable stations for developing upper-body fitness. And it's also a positive way to relieve stress and emotions!

Equipment: Duffle or equipment bag; lots of scrap materials; cord or rope to hang the bag.

Directions:

1. Stuff the duffle bag with styrofoam pieces (these can be stuffed into socks to contain the material), old Nerf™ balls, nylons, old jerseys, chunks of scrap foam, etc. The bag should have a nice give to it when punched.
2. Tape or tie the top of the bag so none of the material pops out when hit.
3. Tie a rope around the top of the bag and loop the other end over a basket support, tree branch, etc., and tie off so that the center of the bag is about chest height for most students. Then let kids punch away!

Tie other end of rope to a strong support. The height of the bag can be changed by retying at a new height.

Suggestion:

❒ Two or three kids can punch at one time with the precaution to punch the bag, *not* each other. The bag will swing so that the punchers will be far enough apart. No hanging on bag. Remind kids to punch, not push.

Variations:

❒ Hugging is, of course, allowed, too!
❒ See "Kick 'n Hit" for a variation of this activity.

7.26 SOCK BALLS

Description: Multi-use balls that are easy to throw and don't hurt when they hit someone. They can be made into various sizes and firmnesses.

Objective: To inexpensively make safe balls for use in many games. These are easy to make and are a good recycling project.

Equipment: Socks; rubber bands; filler material (see "Directions")

Directions: For a soft sockball:

1. Collect long, clean socks.

2. Push any soft material down into the toe of the sock. Pantyhose or nylons give the ball a nice bouncy feel. A second sock or discarded Nerf™ ball or fleece ball will work also and give a different final product.

3. Wrap a rubber band around the sock to keep the shape you want.

4. Fold the sock back onto itself and wrap another rubber band around sock.

5. Continue steps 3 and 4 until you run out of sock, then sew the sock end to the sock ball body to finish.

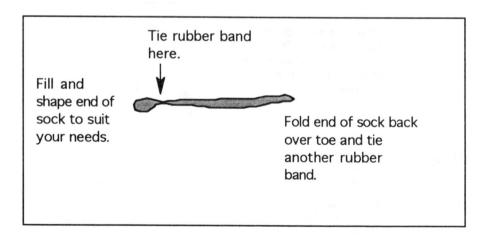

Fill and shape end of sock to suit your needs.

Tie rubber band here.

Fold end of sock back over toe and tie another rubber band.

For a **hard sockball** (suitable for juggling):

1. Use a smaller sock and fill with sand, beans, rice, etc., to the size you want.

2. Follow above directions.

Suggestion:

☐ At Christmas one year I put up a bag and sign that said, "All I want for Christmas are your old socks (clean, of course)." I still have socks left from that request!

7.27 SPORTS TESTER

Description: A station to test knowledge of sports facts.

Objective: Use this station for those students who are unable to participate actively due to injury or illness.

Equipment: 1 clean quart-sized milk carton; tagboard for questions; a 2¼" × 9½" piece of tagboard for the tongue; self-stick vinyl; tape

Directions:

1. Cover the carton with self-stick vinyl to decorate and add durability.
2. Cut slots into carton with sharp knife or razor as shown. Slots are 2½ inches wide by ½-¾ inch deep.
3. Open the top of the milk carton. Slide the "tongue" piece into the answer slot and tape, staple, or glue to the inside back of the tester. Cut off any excess material. (See the illustration.)
4. Add a face to the outside of the tester for personality.
5. Make question cards as shown. Laminating will add durability.

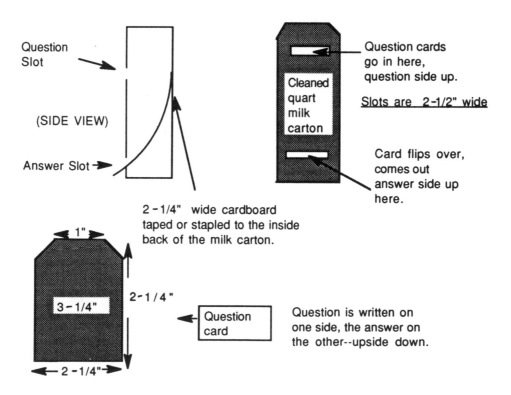

Question Slot

(SIDE VIEW)

Answer Slot ➤

Question cards go in here, question side up.

Cleaned quart milk carton

Slots are 2-1/2" wide

Card flips over, comes out answer side up here.

2-1/4" wide cardboard taped or stapled to the inside back of the milk carton.

1"

3-1/4"

2-1/4"

2-1/4"

Question card

Question is written on one side, the answer on the other--upside down.

Suggestion:

❏ You might also want to make up question cards for just one activity, such as volleyball, and—as a side station—have one team that is not involved in the volleyball game quiz each other on the often-confusing rules of this net game.

Sample Questions and Answers:

1. What was Fat Albert's favorite sport? **(basketball)**

2. What sport has a bullpen? **(baseball)**

3. What's another name for ping pong? **(table tennis)**

4. Name two games that use a totally smooth ball. **(billiards, table tennis, handball, racketball)**

5. Who carries a golfer's clubs? **(a caddie)**

6. What is a full count in baseball? **(3 balls, 2 strikes)**

7. How many bases must you touch when you hit a home run? **(four)**

8. In Australia, soccer is called _____. **(football)**

9. What is a shot in basketball called if it goes in without touching either the rim or the backboard? **(a swish)**

10. What are you doing if you do "Double Dutch"? **(Jumping rope)**

11. What sport has alleys, gutters, and splits? **(bowling)**

12. What sport featured the "Bad News Bears"? **(baseball)**

13. What are the traditional colors on a soccer ball? **(black and white)**

14. Who gobbles up ghosts? **(Pac-man)**

15. If you hit a "Birdie," what sport are you playing? **(badminton)**

16. In which sport do you try for a "knockout"? **(boxing)**

17. Hitting a home run with the bases loaded is called a _____. **(grand slam)**

18. Jumping rope very fast is called _____. **(pepper)**

19. In what sport do you "butterfly"? **(swimming)**

20. In which sport do you "slam dunk"? **(basketball)**

21. What do boxers fight in? **(a ring)**

22. What colors are the three Olympic Medals? **(gold, silver, bronze)**

23. What sport has a gutter ball? **(bowling)**

24. What sport are you playing if someone calls you a "slugger"? **(baseball)**

25. What do hockey players chase around the rink? **(a puck)**

26. What game uses dotted tiles? **(dominoes)**

27. When a team loses without scoring any points or runs, it has been
    _____ _____. **(shut out)**

28. What do relay runners pass from one person to another? **(a baton)**

29. Which football player usually throws the ball? **(the quarterback)**

30. In which sport can you get a hole-in-one? **(golf)**

31. A shot in basketball that touches neither net, rim, or backboard is
    called an _____. **(airball)**

32. All racket sports are started with a _____. **(serve)**

33. Name a sport in which players rotate positions. **(volleyball)**

34. What is the fuzz on a tennis ball called? **(nap)**

35. What golf club is used on the "green"? **(a putter)**

36. For what sport do need a tackle box? **(fishing)**

37. How many miles is a marathon run? **(26)**

38. A perfect score in gymnastics is a _____. **(10)**

39. If a ball lands on a line in a racket sport, is it called in or out? **(in)**

40. The fourth batter in the baseball batting order is called the _____
    _____ **(cleanup hitter)**

41. What sport uses a "pigskin"? **(football)**

42. What sport did Babe Ruth play? **(baseball)**

43. What Olympic sport is played in the water with a net? **(water polo)**

44. What sport has a "high bar"? **(gymnastics, high jump)**

45. What do baseball fans do at the end of the seventh inning? **(stretch)**

46. In which sport are belts important? **(judo, karate)**

47. In football, how many points are scored for a touchdown? **(six)**

48. Zero or no points in tennis is called _____. **(love)**

49. What game starts with a "break"? **(billiards)**

50. What are you doing if you "hang ten"? **(surfing)**

7.28 TOURNAMENT LADDER DISKS

Description: If your classes like tournament play, a simple and effective tournament format for class use is a ladder. Players try to play their way up the ladder as high as they are able, eventually finding others of similar ability level to play against. Ladders can be used in a variety of competitive events, including—but certainly not limited—to:

- Basketball H.O.R.S.E. (try playing "Z.A.P" for faster games)
- Marbles, Jacks
- Racquet sports (like "floor tennis," ping-pong, "Goodminton," etc.)

Objective: To provide a unique way to display students' names in a ladder tournament format.

Equipment: Plastic tennis can lids; magnetic tape; masking tape; tagboard; plastic margarine containers

Directions:

1. Collect plastic tennis can lids, one for each player in the tournament. This may take a while. Enlist the aid of tennis players in the area or ask kids to bring in one disk each. This is also a good way to recycle plastic and clean up areas around tennis courts.

2. Now get a strip of magnetic tape. For each disk, cut two sections of magnet about 1 inch each. Put a piece of masking tape in the center on the **top** of the lid (this helps the magnet stick better). Peel off the paper backing and stick one magnet on *top* of the other in the center of the tennis lid top.

3. Cut pieces of tagboard about 1½" × 1½"; one square for each player. Print the name of one player on each cardboard square.

4. Roll up a small piece of masking tape and stick it to the **bottom** of the tennis lid. Stick the tagboard square to the tape.

5. Place disks on a metal door or other metal surface at the start of the class tournament in random order (see the illustration).

6. Explain the **rules of the ladder** to students:
    a. Players may challenge any of the *three* players above them on the ladder. If they win, they change places with the person they beat.

b. If the challenger loses, the disks stay as they were.

c. Players *must* accept challenges unless they have a good reason, such as already being involved in another challenge match.

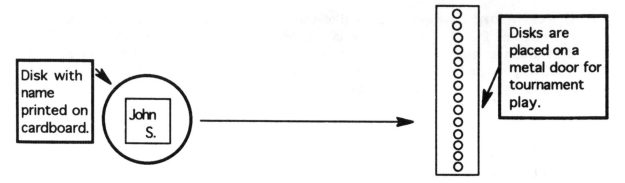

Suggestions:

❑ Disks will stick to any *metal* surfaces like a fire door, metal stripping around a door, etc.

❑ Store these disks in a clean plastic round-tub margarine container. At the end of the day's play, the top player (or the top boy/girl, if playing separately) places the disks into the tub, with the top player ending up on top of the pile, so that they are easy to set up when that class meets again.

❑ Disks are reuseable—just remove the name cards and add new ones next year.

7.29 WRIST ROLLER

Description: An inexpensive piece of exercise equipment for use with all grade levels.

Objective: To develop strength in the upper body, especially the arms.

Equipment: A weight of about 2-4 pounds (a large wooden bowling pin, a small dumbbell, or even a few heavy rubber wheels); strong cord; a handle of about 8-12 inches (a section of broom handle works, as does 1"- 1½ " PVC pipe)

Directions:

1. Tie the weight securely to one end of the cord.
2. Drill a hole through the center of the wood piece or PVC pipe as shown.

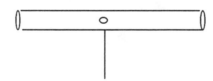

3. Thread cord through the hole and knot the cord so that it will not slip back through the hole.
4. *How to use:* Grasp the bar with arms straight out in front. Roll the handle in your hands so that the cord is wrapped around the handle. Try to roll the cord all the way up and then reverse direction so the weight goes back down.

Suggestion:

❏ Use as a station, either as part of a fitness unit or as a side activity for those not actively playing in a game.

Section 8

ACTIVE SPORTS-DAY DESIGNS

Sports Days are a great way to culminate the school year and the physical education year. Students will look forward to these events, which gives a special meaning to these activities when taught in class.

ACTIVITY INDICATOR

○ Less active

◉ Active

● Very active

Ⓢ Strength

8.1 GENERAL INFORMATION

1. Plan a date late in the school year. Students are familiar with the activities by then, and classroom teachers are more willing to cooperate with changes in their schedules.

2. Plan rain dates (just in case)!

3. Decide whether you want a full-day or a half-day event.

4. Decide on the format or theme. Will you vary the theme of Sports Day or keep the same format year after year? Advantages of using the same format: students become familiar with the events, records can be established, planning is easier. Advantages of changing the format: variety, renewed interest.

5. Meet with volunteers before the actual event. Explain their jobs, how the events are conducted, and the times they will be needed. Older students (or former students) can be called upon to officiate events, if desired. Parents are also a good source for volunteers. (See Section 10 for Volunteer Forms).

6. Organize students into teams or groups. Attempt to make teams of equal overall ability and make sure the boy/girl ratio is equal if they are going to be combined on a team. One possible way to ability-group students is to use scores from a single event, such as the 50-yard dash, to divide teams equally. Give each team an identification—either a name or a color. Colors work especially well because students can be asked to wear that color shirt on Sports Day, thus eliminating the need for jerseys. Have a few jerseys on hand, though, just in case someone forgets.

7. Plan ahead!! Have all equipment ready ahead of time; arrive early on Sports Day to set up.

8. One plan that is beneficial to both your Sports Day and to the classroom teachers is to cancel physical education classes for the week. On each day, a different grade level has its Sports Day, so the classroom teachers have no students for most of the day (except for meeting their classes for a picnic lunch). This allows teachers to work on end-of-the-year classroom obligations. Here is a sample schedule.

Time: 10:00-3:30 *(Lunch 12:00-1:00)*

Monday—Grade 5
Tuesday—Grade 4
Wednesday—Grade 3
Thursday—Grade 2
Friday—Grade 1

NOTE: Scheduling the grade 5's Sports Day first enables some of these students to be used to officiate the events for the younger students as needed.

Be sure to think about:

❐ Water or other refreshments

❐ A megaphone for announcements

❐ Rest room procedures and facilities

❐ Notifying the school nurse, administration, cafeteria staff, and grounds crews

❐ Awards

8.2 OLYMPIC FORMAT

In this Sports Day set-up, students compete against themselves in an attempt to surpass standards to win gold, silver, and bronze medals (paper replicas). Alternately, certificates may be given. Students might also earn points to be totaled for their team score. You might consider embellishing the event with opening and closing ceremonies.

Step 1: Choose the Events for the Competition. Possible selections might include the following individual events:

- ❐ 50-meter dash
- ❐ 50-meter hurdles (see Section 7 under "Hurdles")
- ❐ standing or running long jump
- ❐ high jump
- ❐ pole vault
- ❐ javelin throw
- ❐ hammer throw
- ❐ triathlon
- ❐ shot put (or softball distance throw)
- ❐ discus throw (no discus—try a small hoop or inner tube throw)
- ❐ marathon run (1 mile or distance of choice)
- ❐ Frisbee™ distance throw

Step 2: Set Standards. The teacher sets boys' and girls' standards for each event based on observations of students' performance in classes. For example:

JAVELIN THROW					
	Grade 5	Grade 4	Grade 3	Grade 2	Grade 1
Boys' Gold	25 yds.	23 yds.	21 yds.	18 yds.	15 yds.
Girls' Gold	23 yds.	21 yds.	20 yds.	16 yds.	12 yds.
Boys' Silver	20 yds.	18 yds.	16 yds.	13 yds.	10 yds.
Girls' Silver	18 yds.	16 yds.	14 yds.	11 yds.	8 yds.
Boys' Bronze	15 yds.	13 yds.	11 yds.	9 yds.	7 yds.
Girls' Bronze	12 yds.	10 yds.	9 yds.	7 yds,	6 yrds.

Make the Gold standard reachable for only about 20-25% of the students. Make the Bronze standard unreachable for about 5-10% of students. You want the standards to be challenging, but obtainable.

Step 3: Prepare for Sports Day. Mark the various distances for each event using cones or other markers. To quickly be able to adjust cones from one grade level and/or gender to another, mark the distance on the field or court with a small amount of lime or grass paint. Then set the cone on top of the appropriate mark (or midway between markings). If cones get displaced, they are easily reset. For example:

```
Javelin
Throwing          8'  10' 12' 14' 16' 18' 20' 22' 24'
Line    ────►     •   •   •   •   •   •   •   •   •
                                     ↖ Lime marking
```

An alternate method is to place a measuring tape (or a string knotted each foot) directly on the field or court. If markers on the field are not appropriate to the event (such as the 50-meter dash or the high jump), make up signs that can be posted at the event with the times or heights needed for achieving medals.

Step 4: Group Students.

    a. Number each event consecutively, 1-2-3-, etc.

    b. Divide the total number of students in a grade by the number of events. For example: 60 students/10 events = 6 students per group.

Step 5: Determine Group Rotation.

    a. Have Group #1 start at event #1, Group #2 at event #2, and so on.

    b. When all members of a group have completed an event, they go to the next numbered event, but they must wait for the previous group to finish and move on before beginning the new event.

    c. Plan on approximately 15-25 minutes per event (depending on the number of students per group). Thus, a 10-event Sports Day will require about 2½ to 4 hours.

Step 6: Gather Volunteers. Enlist parents, older students, or other volunteers to conduct each event. The physical education teacher acts as the facilitator, seeing to any problems that may arise. The volunteers need to see that students participate safely and accurately in the events and also award medals to those achieving the standards. Meet these workers before the actual events to go over duties, times, procedures, etc. (See Section 10 for a Volunteer Form.)

Step 7: Conduct the Events.

a. Allow students two or more chances to reach their highest score in an event.

b. Award the appropriate medal, if the standard is met. Medals are reprints that can be run off in large numbers. (See Section 10.) Purchased award ribbons or certificates may also be used.

c. Award points to each individual's team if a team total is to be kept.

Suggestions:

❐ If your school doesn't have enough cones, plastic milk jugs work fine for marking events. You will need six jugs or cones per event: Gold, Silver, Bronze for both boys and girls. In fact, the jugs can be painted gold, silver, and bronze so students can see the actual distance they need to achieve. Fill each jug with a little sand or water to make more stable.

8.3 ACTIVE GAMES FORMAT

Students compete as teams in various games.

Step 1: Choose the Events. Select events that appeal to your students and are relatively simple to officiate and to organize. Possible choices:

Grades 1-3	*Grades 4-8*
Smurf Dodge	Aerobic Frisbee™
Grass Dodge	Keepaway
Tug-o-War	Tug-o-War
Never Out	Never Out
Pac-man	Postball
Scooter Basketball	Swatball
Scooter Dodge	Team Handball
Tree Tag	Pin Bombardment
Parachute Fun	Modified Lacrosse
Ghost Busters	Whiffleball or Softball
"New Games" Ideas	Shuttle Hurdle Relay

Step 2: Divide the Students into Teams. Dividing each grade level into three or four teams works best. You want about 10-14 students per team. Assign a color to each team and ask them to wear that color shirt on Sports Day. See Step 4 of Olympic Format for an equitable way of dividing into teams. NOTE: Some games will require all team members playing at once, others only a certain number. If, for instance, there are 13 on a team, but only 8 are used in the game, teams will play 8 and substitute at intervals. If a game requires all players, the teams must be equal in number. So, if one team has 13 and the opponent 11, both teams would field 11 players, with the first team having two substitutes.

Step 3: Decide How Competitive Your Sports Day Will Be. With primary grades it may be advisable to have all games played just for fun, with no team score, awards, etc. With older children, the more you keep team scores and give out awards, the more competitive the events will be.

Step 4: Set Up a Schedule of Events. The following is a sample all-day Sports Day for grade 5 with four teams:

First Session	10:00-10:15 10:20-10:35 10:40-10:55	Boys' Keepaway Boys' Keepaway Boys' Keepaway	Red vs. Yellow Green vs. Blue Winner vs. Winner
	10:00-10:15 10:20-10:35 10:40-10:55	Girls' Dodge Girls' Dodge Girls' Dodge	Yellow vs. Green Red vs. Blue Winner vs. Winner
Second Session	11:00-11:15 11:20-11:35	Boys' Tug-o-war Boys' Shuttle Hurdle Relay	Green vs. Yellow Blue vs. Red Winner vs. Winner
	11:00-11:15 11:20-11:35	Girls' Shuttle Hurdle Relay Girls' Tug-o-war	Yellow vs. Red Blue vs. Green Winner vs. Winner
	11:40-12:20	*Lunch with the classroom teacher.*	
Third Session	12:20-12:35 12:40-12:55	Boys' Soccer Boys' Soccer	Green vs. Blue Red vs. Yellow
	12:20-12:35 12:40-12:55	Girls' Keepaway Girls' Keepaway	Red vs. Green Blue vs. Yellow
Fourth Session	1:00- 1:15 1:20- 1:35 1:40- 1:55	Boys' Dodge Boys' Dodge Boys' Dodge	Blue vs. Yellow Green vs. Red Winner vs. Winner
	1:00- 1:20 1:25- 1:45	Girls' Soccer Girls' Soccer	Yellow vs. Red Blue vs. Green
Ffith Session	2:00- 2:20 2:25- 2:45	Boys' Whiffle Ball Boys' Whiffle Ball	Red vs. Yellow Blue vs. Green
	2:00- 2:20 2:25- 2:45	Girls' Never Out Girls' Never Out	Yellow vs. Green Blue vs. Red
Sixth Session	2:50- 3:05 3:10- 3:25	Boys' Never Out Boys' Never Out	Blue vs. Red Green vs. Yellow
	2:50- 3:05 3:10- 3:25	Girls' Whiffle Ball Girls' Whiffle Ball	Green vs. Blue Yellow vs. Red
	3:30	*Closing Remarks and/or Ceremonies.*	

Suggestions:

❐ Each activity does not have to conclude with a championship game. Some games require a longer time period and leave no time for a championship.

❐ Play tug-o-war in a sand area, if possible. Contests last longer, and are safer and more fun than on grass.

❐ The five minutes between sessions allow for drink and bathroom breaks and reorganization of groups.

❐ The choice of events and time allotments are all adjustable.

❐ Any group not actively involved can assist with officiating or take a rest/bathroom/drink break.

FITNESS TESTING

Fitness testing can be initiated as early as age five. Students, teachers, and parents can use the results of these tests to evaluate fitness progress, assess individual needs, and determine personal goals.

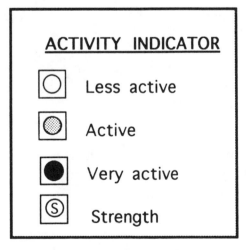

ACTIVITY INDICATOR

◯ Less active

◉ Active

● Very active

Ⓢ Strength

FITNESS TESTING

The purpose of evaluating physical fitness should be to show students their areas of strength and the other areas that might need work in relation to their fitness level. Why wait until high school or later to discover that a student's flexibility or cardio-vascular fitness is below established standards? Children at the elementary level are especially interested in learning about fitness and will make efforts to improve future fitness scores.

The fitness test I've used for a number of years is a combination of several national tests that have norms beginning at age five. I developed this test because it's easy to administer and students seem to enjoy the activities. The test measures the three major strength areas, as well as flexibility and cardio-vascular fitness. The five test items are described below. The reporting forms, with norms, are included in Section 10. Body composition is omitted from this test despite its importance as a fitness concern. Body fat is difficult to test accurately, time-consuming, and possibly embarrassing; therefore, it is not included in this evaluation.

❐ **Situps** test *abdominal muscle fitness*. Strong stomach muscles are important in virtually every athletic movement, critical to good posture, and vital for protecting internal organs.

Procedure: The performer lies on a mat with knees bent so that the heels are about 15 inches from the buttocks. The arms are folded across the chest with the hands on the opposite shoulders. A partner holds down the performer's feet and also acts as the counter. A correct sit-up is completed when the performer touches his or her elbows to the knees and returns the back to the mat, keeping the buttocks in contact with the mat. The partner counts the number of sit-ups completed in 60 seconds. Pauses are allowed.

❐ **Sit and Reach** evaluates *flexibility*. This is a standard test that measures lower back and hamstring flexibility. Being flexible allows one's body greater range of motion and decreases the likelihood of injury. For the average person, extreme flexibility and extreme tightness are both to be avoided.

Procedure: The student sits on the floor or mat with legs extended. Shoes may be removed for more accurate scoring, but this is not absolutely essential. The teacher can ensure that a student's legs remain straight by pushing down on one or both knees. The feet are placed against a box or bench so that the student can reach past the toes. The student places both hands together, or one on top of the other, and slowly stretches forward as far as possible. There should be no bouncing. Tape a yardstick to the bench so that the 9 inch mark is even with the vertical plane of the feet.

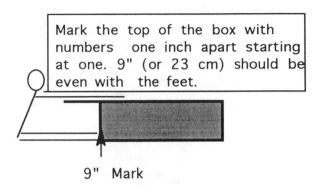

Mark the top of the box with numbers one inch apart starting at one. 9" (or 23 cm) should be even with the feet.

9" Mark

☐ **Standing Long Jump** evaluates *leg power*. This test is best done on a mat in order to cushion the landing. The teacher might want to mark a mat with magic marker for a permanent jumping mat, as shown. Alongside the appropriate distance, indicate that the score is an age group norm. (Example: alongside 3'7" indicate *Girls Age 7*.) See Section 10 for details on making a Long Jump Mat.

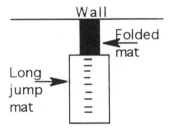

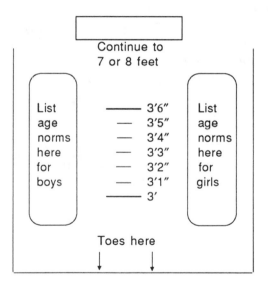

*Do not place the long jump mat directly against a wall since students may stumble forward after their jump. Place a folded mat against the wall to keep the long jump mat farther from the wall.

Procedure: Students should be shown the technique of long jumping and be given practice time. (See "Blast Off" in Section 4.) Allow students several turns—then record the best score. Measure the jump from whatever body part touches nearest the starting point, whether it be the heels of the feet, the hands, etc.

❐ **Endurance Run** assesses *cardio-vascular fitness*. Measure the running course on a flat, smooth grassy area or a hard-surface court. Prepare students for the test by including vigorous activities in the weeks prior to the test and by discussions about pacing. Avoid extremely cold, hot, or windy days for the test.

❐ **Bent Arm Bar Hang** evaluates *upper body strength*. The bent arm hang is used because almost all students will be able to record a score. If chin-ups were used, almost half of the students would not record a score. The *overhand grip* is used because more muscle groups are brought into use, and it more closely correlates to other athletic movements than the underhand grip.

Procedure: Set the chinning bar just high enough so that the performer's feet will not touch the floor. If the bar is too high, fear may be a factor in the score, and safety also may be compromised. When the performer gets into position with the chin just over the bar, but not touching the bar, and the legs are hanging down straight, the teacher starts the timer's watch. Stop the watch when the performer's chin comes to rest on the bar or the chin drops below the bar. Do not allow the performer to swing.

How to Administer the Test: Most test items are best taught to the class as a whole, then set up as a station for testing. For instance, while some students are playing indoor hockey or soccer, the teacher tests others on flexibility or the bar hang. The endurance run is best tested as a whole class activity.

After testing is completed, fill out a Fitness Report (see Section 10) for each student, and distribute. Be sure to copy the information to parents on the opposite side of students' scores. Encourage students and parents to keep the scores for future reference.

Discuss ways in which students can improve their scores. Also discuss the meaning of each test. If time allows, a follow-up retest gives students the opportunity to improve their scores. A special certificate might be given to any student who scores average or above in all five test items, or to students who demonstrated appreciable improvement since their last evaluation.

READY-TO-USE FORMS

Included in this section are prepared, ready-to-use forms that will save time and effort when using an activity. Why make up a new form each year when you can just copy the forms you need?

ACTIVITY INDICATOR

○	Less active
◔	Active
●	Very active
Ⓢ	Strength

TIMER'S CHECK SHEET FOR ½ MILE RUN

Place one check (√) to the left of the time for each runner.

← ADDITIONAL TIMES

	2:44	3:26	4:08	4:50
	:45	:27	:09	:51
	:46	:28	:10	:52
	:47	:29	:11	:53
	:48	:30	:12	:54
	:49	:31	:13	:55
	:50	:32	:14	:56
	:51	:33	:15	:57
	:52	:34	:16	:58
	:53	:35	:17	:59
	:54	:36	:18	**5:00**
	:55	:37	:19	:01
	:56	:38	:20	:02
	:57	:39	:21	:03
	:58	:40	:22	:04
	:59	:41	:23	:05
	3:00	:42	:24	:06
	:01	:43	:25	:07
2:20	:02	:44	:26	:08
:21	:03	:45	:27	:09
:22	:04	:46	:28	:10
:23	:05	:47	:29	:11
:24	:06	:48	:30	:12
:25	:07	:49	:31	:13
:26	:08	:50	:32	:14
:27	:09	:51	:33	:15
:28	:10	:52	:34	:16
:29	:11	:53	:35	:17
:30	:12	:54	:36	:18
:31	:13	:55	:37	:19
:32	:14	:56	:38	:20
:33	:15	:57	:39	
:34	:16	:58	:40	
:35	:17	:59	:41	
:36	:18	**4:00**	:42	
:37	:19	:01	:43	
:38	:20	:02	:44	
:39	:21	:03	:45	
:40	:22	:04	:46	
:41	:23	:05	:47	
:42	:24	:06	:48	
:43	:25	:07	:49	

← ADDITIONAL TIMES

TIMER'S CHECK SHEET FOR 1 MILE RUN

Place one check (√) to the left of the time for each runner.						
5:00	5:46	6:30	7:14	7:58	8:42	9:26
:01	:47	:31	:15	:59	:43	:27
:02	:48	:32	:16	**8:00**	:44	:28
:03	:49	:33	:17	:01	:45	:29
:04	:50	:34	:18	:02	:46	:30
:05	:51	:35	:19	:03	:47	:31
:06	:52	:36	:20	:04	:48	:32
:07	:53	:37	:21	:05	:49	:33
:08	:54	:38	:22	:06	:50	:34
:09	:55	:39	:23	:07	:51	:35
:10	:56	:40	:24	:08	:52	:36
:11	:57	:41	:25	:09	:53	:37
:12	:58	:42	:26	:10	:54	:38
:13	:59	:43	:27	:11	:55	:39
:14	**6:00**	:44	:28	:12	:56	:40
:15	:01	:45	:29	:13	:57	:41
:16	:02	:46	:30	:14	:58	:42
:17	:03	:47	:31	:15	:59	:43
:18	:04	:48	:32	:16	**9:00**	:44
:19	:05	:49	:33	:17	:01	:45
:20	:06	:50	:34	:18	:02	:46
:21	:07	:51	:35	:19	:03	:47
:22	:08	:52	:36	:20	:04	:48
:23	:09	:53	:37	:21	:05	:49
:24	:10	:54	:38	:22	:06	:50
:25	:11	:55	:39	:23	:07	:51
:26	:12	:56	:40	:24	:08	:52
:27	:13	:57	:41	:25	:09	:53
:28	:14	:58	:42	:26	:10	:54
:29	:15	:59	:43	:27	:11	:55
:30	:16	**7:00**	:44	:28	:12	:56
:31	:17	:01	:45	:29	:13	:57
:32	:18	:02	:46	:30	:14	:58
:33	:19	:03	:47	:31	:15	:59
:34	:20	:04	:48	:32	:16	**10:00**
:35	:21	:05	:49	:33	:17	
:36	:22	:06	:50	:34	:18	O
:37	:23	:07	:51	:35	:19	T →
:38	:24	:08	:52	:36	:20	H
:39	:25	:09	:53	:37	:21	E
:40	:26	:10	:54	:38	:22	R
:41	:27	:11	:55	:39	:23	
:42	:28	:12	:56	:40	:24	T
:43	:29	:13	:57	:41	:25	I →
:44						M
:45						E
						S

FITNESS TEST REPORT

The purpose of this fitness screening is to point out areas of strengths and other areas that might need improvement in physical fitness. It is not intended to compare one student with another, but rather with national averages for each age. Body size and build will certainly affect scores, as will motivation and general health.

Take a positive approach toward improving any exceptionally weak areas. Children at these ages should not be on a strictly regulated training program, but rather should be encouraged to be more physically active for fun as well as for fitness.

During physical education classes, students will be shown ways to improve scores and activities to practice at home. Any encouragement or assistance from parents will further the likelihood of each child achieving and maintaining physical fitness.

FITNESS TEST REPORT

The purpose of this fitness screening is to point out areas of strengths and other areas that might need improvement in physical fitness. It is not intended to compare one student with another, but rather with national averages for each age. Body size and build will certainly affect scores, as will motivation and general health.

Take a positive approach toward improving any exceptionally weak areas. Children at these ages should not be on a strictly regulated training program, but rather should be encouraged to be more physically active for fun as well as for fitness.

During physical education classes, students will be shown ways to improve scores and activities to practice at home. Any encouragement or assistance from parents will further the likelihood of each child achieving and maintaining physical fitness.

FITNESS TEST REPORT

Name:_____ 🏃 Age:_____

	TEST	Your Score	**National Norms**						
			Age 6	Age 7	Age 8	Age 9	Age 10	Age 11	Age 12
G	60-Second Sit-ups (abdominal strength)		22	25	29	29	32	34	36
I	Sit and Reach (flexibility)		10"	10"	10"	10"	10"	10"	10"
R	Standing Long Jump (leg power)		3'3"	3'7"	3'11"	4'3"	4'8"	4'11"	5'0"
L	Endurance Run (cardio-vascular fitness)		¼ Mile		½ Mile		One Mile		
			2:32	2:29	5:04	5:00	11:30	10:27	9:47
S	Bar Hang (upper body strength)		5 sec.	5 sec.	8 sec.	8 sec.	8 sec.	8 sec.	8 sec.

FITNESS TEST REPORT

Name:_____ 🏃 Age:_____

	TEST	Your Score	**National Norms**						
			Age 6	Age 7	Age 8	Age 9	Age 10	Age 11	Age 12
B	60-Second Sit-ups (abdominal strength)		20	26	30	32	34	37	39
O	Sit and Reach (flexibility)		10"	10"	10"	10"	10"	10"	10"
Y	Standing Long Jump (leg power)		3'7"	3'11"	4'3"	4'9"	4'11"	5'2"	5'5"
S	Endurance Run (cardio-vascular fitness)		¼ Mile		½ Mile		One Mile		
			2:24	2:20	4:30	4:26	11:00	9:06	8:20
	Bar Hang (upper body strength)		5 sec.	5 sec.	10 sec.	10 sec.	10 sec.	10 sec.	10 sec.

FRISBEE™ GOLF

BASKETBALL GOLF

FRISBEE™ GOLF

BASKETBALL GOLF

NAMES →					NAMES →				
HOLE #1					HOLE #1				
HOLE #2					HOLE #2				
HOLE #3					HOLE #3				
HOLE #4					HOLE #4				
HOLE #5					HOLE #5				
HOLE #6					HOLE #6				
HOLE #7					HOLE #7				
HOLE #8					HOLE #8				
HOLE #9					HOLE #9				
TOTALS →					TOTALS →				

MULTI-START RACE (Form #1)

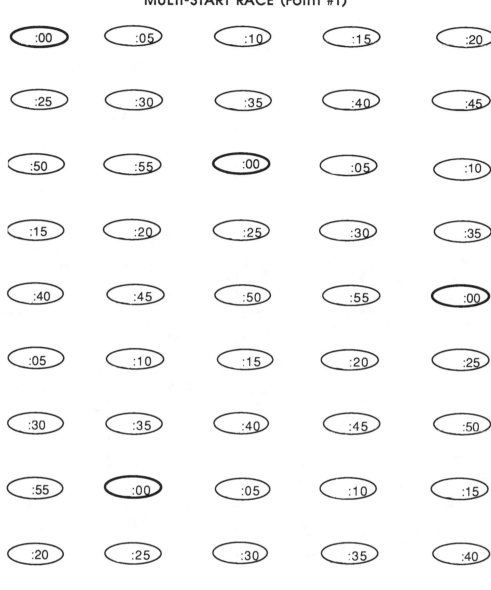

:00 :05 :10 :15 :20

:25 :30 :35 :40 :45

:50 :55 :00 :05 :10

:15 :20 :25 :30 :35

:40 :45 :50 :55 :00

:05 :10 :15 :20 :25

:30 :35 :40 :45 :50

:55 :00 :05 :10 :15

:20 :25 :30 :35 :40

:45 :50 :55 :00 :05

Instructions for Use:

❏ Place the number of minutes in the circles provided, beginning with the fastest time from Run #1.

❏ Place the names of students below the time that is *closest* to what they ran in the previous run. There may be several names under a given time.

MULTI-START RACE (Form #2)

ORDER OF STARTING				
	:0	1:00	2:00	3:00
	:05	1:05	2:05	3:05
	:10	1:10	2:10	3:10
	:15	1:15	2:15	3:15
	:20	1:20	2:20	3:20
	:25	1:25	2:25	3:25
	:30	1:30	2:30	3:30
	:35	1:35	2:35	3:35
	:40	1:40	2:40	3:40
	:45	1:45	2:45	3:45
	:50	1:50	2:50	3:50
	:55	1:55	2:55	3:55

Instructions for Use: Take the names from Form #1 and place them in reverse order on this form (with slowest now being first). Names are spaced in relation to their times in the first race. The slowest runner in the first race starts in the first space (marked "0").

MILE RUN+

These students have

run more than **ONE MILE** nonstop !

MILE RUN

The following students have successfully

run **ONE MILE** without stopping.

*Cut out these headings to place over your running charts.

Section Ten / READY-TO-USE FORMS

247

PERMISSION LETTER FOR AFTER-SCHOOL RUNS

Dear Parents/Guardians:

This fall your child will have the opportunity to participate in several "cross country" running events with children from other schools in the area. The approximate distance of these events is one mile. Students have been participating in vigorous activities in class and are prepared to complete the distance.

The purposes in making this opportunity available are:

- ❒ to encourage running as a means of both fun and fitness
- ❒ to expose children from different communities to a healthy and challenging competition in a supportive environment
- ❒ to experience the joy of participating in and completing a challenging activity

These events are offered on a voluntary basis and are open to all children in grades _____. **The schedule and entry forms for these events are on the other side of this notice.** Transportation to and from the events must be provided by the parents/guardians.

If you would like your child to participate in any or all of these events, please fill in the appropriate entry form and return to _____ _____. If you have any questions, please contact your teacher at school.

Thank you for your interest and cooperation.

Sincerely,

_____

Suggestions:

Runners should:

- ❒ Wear appropriate shoes and clothing for distance running.
- ❒ Bring water to drink and warm clothing to wear after the run.
- ❒ Arrive early in order to register and to prepare for the run.

ENTRY FORM/PERMISSION SLIP

The student named below has my permission to participate in the cross country meet (approximately one mile distance) on _____ at _____ School.   Rain Date: _____

Name_____   Grade_____

I understand that I am responsible for transportation arrangements.

Parent/Guardian Signature:_____

ENTRY FORM/PERMISSION SLIP

The student named below has my permission to participate in the cross country meet (approximately one mile distance) on _____ at _____ School.   Rain Date: _____

Name_____   Grade_____

I understand that I am responsible for transportation arrangements.

Parent/Guardian Signature:_____

ENTRY FORM/PERMISSION SLIP

The student named below has my permission to participate in the cross country meet (approximately one mile distance) on _____ at _____ School.   Rain Date: _____

Name_____   Grade_____

I understand that I am responsible for transportation arrangements.

Parent/Guardian Signature:_____

This Certificate is Awarded To

_____

For Outstanding Achievement

in

JUGGLING

_____ Date

_____ Teacher

_____ Grade

VOLUNTEER FORM FOR SPORTS DAYS

_____
(Name of School)

We are looking for volunteers to help conduct this year's Sports Days. The schedule is as follows:

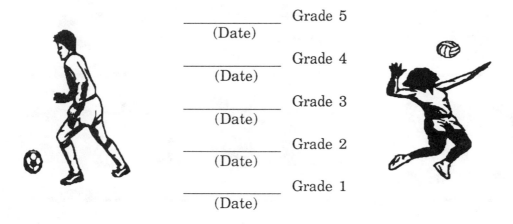

_____ Grade 5
(Date)

_____ Grade 4
(Date)

_____ Grade 3
(Date)

_____ Grade 2
(Date)

_____ Grade 1
(Date)

These events are a lot of fun for the kids and for the volunteers. But we need assistance to run the events. If you can help, please tear off the attached form and return to school by _____.

We will need to meet with all volunteers to discuss the events. We will notify you at a later date of the time and location of this meeting.

Tear off and return this form.

_____ I would like to help on Sports Days.

_____ are the date(s) that I can help.

_____   _____
Name of Volunteer   Phone Number

© 1993 by Parker Publishing Company

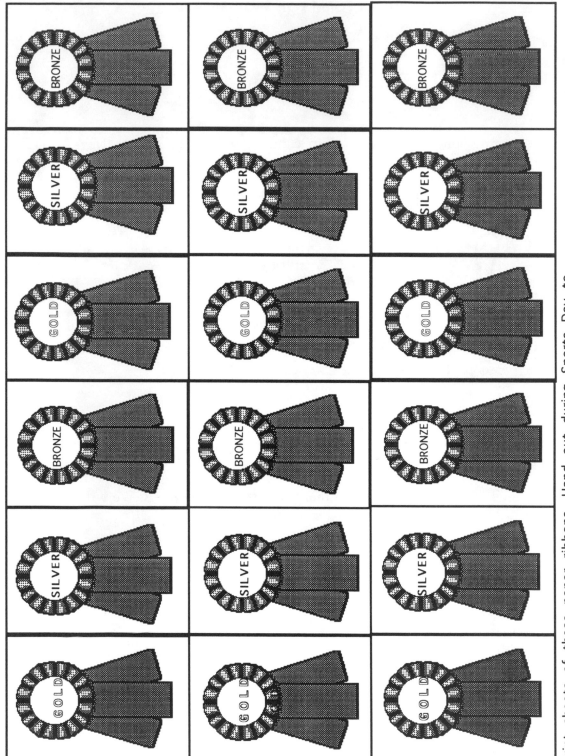

Print sheets of these paper ribbons. Hand out during Sports Day to students achieving the standards.

Section Ten / READY-TO-USE FORMS

LIST OF ACTIVITIES